SEVEN PROPHETS
AND THE CULTURE WAR

Undoing the Philosophies
of a World in Crisis

Copyright © 2024 by Alexandre Havard

The total or partial reproduction of this book is not permitted, not its informatic treatment, or the transmission of any form or by any means, either electronic, mechanic, photocopy or other methods, without the prior written permission of the publisher.

Asterisks in the footnotes are used to indicate English rendering of a foreign-language title with no published English translation. Translation by Anthony Salvia.

Published by Scepter Publishers, Inc.
info@scepterpublishers.org
www.scepterpublishers.org
800-322-8773
New York

All rights reserved.

Cover by Marc Whitaker, MTW Design
Text design and pagination by Rose Design

Cover photo: Alamy stock photo by Brain Light

Library of Congress Control Number: 2023940558

ISBN: 978-1-59417-506-0 (pbk)
ISBN: 978-1-59417-507-7 (ebook)

Printed in the United States of America

SEVEN PROPHETS AND THE CULTURE WAR

Undoing the Philosophies of a World in Crisis

Translated from French by Anthony Salvia

ALEXANDRE HAVARD

Scepter

CONTENTS

Preface ix

Part 1: THE DESTROYERS

1. The Rationalism of René Descartes
   (1596–1650) 3
2. Jean-Jacques Rousseau's Sentimentalism
   (1712–1778) 18
3. Friedrich Nietzsche's Voluntarism
   (1844–1900) 38

Part 2: THE BUILDERS

1. Blaise Pascal's Reasons of the Heart
   (1623–1662) 57
2. The Authentic Life of Sören Kierkegaard
   (1813–1855) 81
3. The Humanity of Fyodor Dostoyevsky
   (1821–1881) 96
4. The Unified Life of Vladimir Soloviev
   (1853–1900) 126

Conclusion 155

Three of the seven "prophets" we present in this book—Descartes, Rousseau, and Nietzsche—provoked or facilitated, through their intellectual activity, great upheavals. The others—Pascal, Kierkegaard, Dostoyevsky, and Soloviev—predicted these very upheavals but showed us the way to overcome them. If we study all seven of them in depth, we will have an easier time grasping the essence and origin of the universal drama now unfolding before our eyes and making wise and courageous choices for a better future.

PREFACE

"AS LONG AS THIS STATE ENDURES, one is, like God, sufficient unto oneself."[1] I was a sixteen-year-old high school student when I heard these words of Jean-Jacques Rousseau for the first time. I found them vile and despicable and would repeat them every time I crossed the threshold of the school bathroom. I realized that many talented people—every day, every hour, every second—were drowning in the swamp of self-sufficiency.

I remember our philosophy teacher in my senior year. He told us about the insights of Descartes, Kant, and Hegel: "A beautiful sunset, dear students, exists in reality only if it exists beforehand in your thoughts. Without man's thought, nothing exists. Being is the fruit of thought. There is no reality apart from the thought of the thinking subject; the rest is only the product of this thought." Although still a teenager and not having seen the movie *The Matrix* (it came out twenty years later), I well understood that in making assertions of this kind, we were going beyond self-sufficiency and entering a state of insanity.

But when, a few months later, in 1979, I came across these words by Albert Camus in our philosophy

---

1. J.-J. Rousseau, *Reveries of the Solitary Walker* (1782), fifth walk.

textbook, namely, "Consciousness comes into the world with revolt,"[2] I experienced a burst of joy and optimism. Camus' words signaled to me the revolt against oneself, against the spiritual indifference that devours us.

The influence of philosophy on our lives—on education, culture, politics, society in general—is undeniable. Plato inspired the Christian world in large part until the thirteenth century; Aristotle and Thomas Aquinas together inspired Europeans from the thirteenth to the seventeenth century; modern civilization is fundamentally the product of Descartes' thought; in the twentieth century, Marx considerably influenced the behavior of the world's elites and the destiny of many nations; Nietzsche is still today the point of reference for all who aspire to "superhumanity," to the violent affirmation of the "I"; and Rousseau is the intellectual father of a multitude of pseudo-religions which for two hundred years have been trying with surprising success to substitute themselves for Christianity.

Philosophers produce ideas that invade our hearts and minds—for good or for ill. It is important to understand these ideas, and to unravel them to determine what is true about them and what is false, which ones elevate man, and which ones debase him. But it is even more important to determine *what manner of person* is the philosopher who is speaking to us.

"Immanuel Kant's life story," wrote the German poet Heinrich Heine, "is difficult to describe, because he had

---

2. A. Camus, *L'homme Révolté*, 133e édition, collection NRF (Paris: Les Éditions Gallimard, 1951), p. 20.

neither a life nor a story."³ A philosopher without life and without history—is such a philosopher credible? Is his philosophy viable?

We like to debate the ideas of this or that philosopher, but too often we leave out the study of his personality. We are interested in what the philosopher says, not in what he is. This is a very serious mistake, because behind ideas there is a heart, and if this heart is "rotten," the ideas will be rotten too, and the one who imbibes such ideas will end up rotten himself. The opposite is also true: the powerful and true ideas of some philosophers are often the expression of a noble and magnanimous heart which communicates to us the vital inspiration we need to purify ourselves, to elevate ourselves, and to reach the heights of our humanity.

This book begins with Descartes (1596–1650) who is undoubtedly the father of modern philosophy. Descartes needed certainty, which is natural for a man of science. But to achieve this result, he created a method according to which thought is the only criterion of certainty: "I think, therefore I am." His belief: my existence is proven by the fact that I think. If I stopped thinking, the evidence of my existence would disappear. Therefore, I exist when I think, and only when I think. Descartes reduces being to thinking.

---

3. T. Pinkard, "Preface to the Second Edition, in T. Pinkard, ed., *Heine: "On the History of Religion and Philosophy in Germany,"* trans. H. Pollack-Milgate, Cambridge Texts in the History of Philosophy (Cambridge: Cambridge University Press, 2007), doi.org/10.1017/CBO9780511808043.006, pp. 4–118.

His "I think, therefore I am" inevitably becomes "I am, because I think." For Hegel, who will finish Descartes' work, thought ceases to be the proof of being: it becomes the cause of being, it produces being. Descartes probably did not understand where his philosophy would lead. By making thought the only criterion of certainty, however, he plunged humanity into the most absolute subjectivism.

The first part of this book considers those I call *the destroyers*: Descartes, Rousseau, and Nietzsche. In studying their lives and their thought, it seems clear that two of the three spiritual centers of man—the heart, the intellect, and the will—have atrophied in each of these philosophers. In Descartes, the heart and the will are strangled by *reason*; in Rousseau, reason and the will are suffocated by the *heart*; in Nietzsche, reason and the heart are absorbed by the *will*. Descartes embodies rationalism; Rousseau, sentimentalism; Nietzsche, voluntarism.

Descartes, who was not religiously minded but outwardly observed the rites of Christianity, created a way of thinking that was incompatible with the Christian faith. Without wanting to, he became the father of modern atheism. Rousseau, who had a religious spirit but did not believe in Jesus Christ, fashioned a parody of Christianity that was as infamous as it was seductive. Nietzsche, anti-religious and anti-Christian, produced the cruel and dramatic image of the "superman," the antithesis of the God-man of the Christian religion.

Descartes, Rousseau, and Nietzsche are founders. Kant and Hegel are only the logical continuation of Descartes: they elaborate systems on the basis of the Cartesian idea. Although they possess intellects of exceptional power, their originality is only "secondary." For this reason, we shall deal with neither Kant nor Hegel here.

Nor shall we refer to Karl Marx, the intellectual heir to Rousseau, in the body of our text, but because Marxism was the dominant ideology of the twentieth century, let us say a few words about him in this preface.

Like Rousseau, Marx was religious but unlike Rousseau, he believed in Jesus Christ—so much so that he declared war on him. Marx, baptized into the Lutheran Church at the age of six, became a satanist. He wrote "satanic verses," published during his lifetime in the German magazine *Athenäum*: "The hellish vapors rise and fill the brain, till I go mad and my heart is utterly changed. See this sword? The prince of darkness sold it to me."[4]

Robert Payne and Richard Wurmbrand point to other poems by Marx that are equally explicit:

> Thus, heaven I've forfeited, I know it full well / My soul, once true to God / Is chosen for hell . . . / Nothing but revenge is left to me. / I shall build my throne high overhead, / Cold, tremendous shall its

---

4. K. Marx, *Der Spielmann* (Player, also translated as The Fiddler), written in 1837 and published in *Athenäum: Zeitschrift für das gebildete Deutschland*, January 23, 1841.

summit be . . . / Soon I shall embrace eternity to my breast, and soon I shall howl gigantic curses on mankind . . . / With disdain I will throw my gauntlet full in the face of the world / And see the collapse of this pygmy giant [i.e., Christ] / Whose fall will not stifle my ardor. / Then will I wander godlike and victorious / Through the ruins of the world / And, giving my words an active force, / I will feel equal to the Creator."[5]

Nietzsche called himself the "Antichrist," but that was a red herring because he did not believe in Christ at all. Marx, on the other hand, is a true antichrist. He is the "personal enemy of God" (as Lenin called himself). Marxism is a weapon created by Karl Marx to finish with God. Marx believed in Marxism as one believes in the instrument, but naturally did *not* believe in Marxist "science": in an earthly paradise in a communist state without religion, without family, without private property. Marx cynically mocked God and humanity. He didn't care about the proletariat; he dreamed of ending Judeo-Christian civilization. Marxism is a demonic phenomenon brilliantly depicted by Dostoyevsky in his novel *The Devils* (1872) during Marx's own lifetime.

"Socialism," wrote Nikolai Berdyaev in 1906, "claims to become the religion of the new humanity, its intrinsic

---

5. R. Payne, *The Unknown Karl Marx* (New York: New York University Press, 1971), p. 12; R. Wurmbrand, *Was Marx a Satanist?* (1986), pp. 9, 12, 15, 22.

link with religion unquestionable."⁶ "Socialism is a messianism," continues the Russian philosopher,

> the proletariat is the new Israel. . . . The chosen class establishes on earth the promised kingdom, it offers the happiness that the Crucified Messiah did not bring. The proletariat is the new Messiah, the founder of an earthly kingdom in the name of which the old Messiah was rejected, who announced a kingdom which "is not of this world." . . . The transfer of power to this new class constitutes the great historical leap towards freedom, the world revolution after which true history or metahistory will begin.⁷

Marxism has passed,⁸ but it was only one of the multiple variants of Rousseauism. Rousseau, the intellectual

---

6. N. Berdiaev, Н.Бердяев, *Социализм как религия*. Вопросы философии и психологии (Socialism as religion, in *Questions of Philosophy and Psychology**) (Moscow, 1906), translation from Russian, http://www.odinblago.ru/filosofiya/berdyaev/berdyaev_socializm_relig/.

7. N. Berdiaev, Н. Бердяев, *Демократия, социализм и теократия. Берлин* (Democracy, socialism, and theocracy, in *The New Middle Ages**) (Berlin, 1924), translation from Russian, http://hrono.ru/libris/lib_b/berd08.html.

8. With the collapse of the Soviet Union in 1991, Marxism as an economic doctrine took a major hit though it lives on in various guises in various places. But Marxism as a moral doctrine (part of Karl Marx's satanic agenda) remains vibrantly alive. In the 1960's, under the influence of Marxist thinker Antonio Gramsci's call for a "long march through the institutions," Marxism began placing a heightened emphasis on culture—the universities, news media, organized religion, and the arts, especially film and television. Capitalism, having absorbed the nihilistic Communist notion that good is whatever advances the cause of progressive humanity and evil whatever

father of all modern pseudo-religions, remains surprisingly relevant today.

Descartes, Rousseau, and Nietzsche indelibly marked the world we live in today. It is a *subjectivist* world (Descartes) led by power-hungry "supermen" (Nietzsche) in an atmosphere of *sentimentalist* and *totalitarian* religiosity (Rousseau).

> *Subjectivism.* Being depends on my thought. Being is subjective. So are truth and the good. Being, truth, and the good are "constructions" of my thinking. There is no objective existence, no objective truth, no objective good. I am a pure subject: there are no principles of human nature. There is no human nature. There is no such thing as a human being. There is only my thought. Since there is no objective truth nor objective good, I demand "tolerance" for all my ideas, my opinions, my whims.
>
> *Sentimentalism.* If ideas and values are relative, if there is nothing greater than me, the only thing that can make me happy is myself, my emotions. I have no other rule of life than my sensitivity. My sensitivity is my religion.
>
> *Totalitarianism.* (The dominant ideology of our time, for which there is no commonly agreed term but

---

impedes it, has been trying to erase religion from society ever since, using all of the means at its disposal. The sexual revolution, including its handmaid—gender ideology—are fundamental manifestations of cultural Marxism. Cultural Marxism, like Soviet Marxism, is a pseudo-religion.

which we might call, for the sake of argument, *moral relativism*, to which acquisitive capitalism willingly submit). Mass communication manages my sensitivity and stimulates my emotions. I like it. It makes me feel as though I exist. Distinguishing between truth and falsehood in the information I receive is an exercise in futility, since everything is subjective. And others who stand in the way of my happiness, claiming to impose on me ideas and values which they call "objective," I actively seek to "cancel."

These are the fruits of the philosophy of Descartes, Rousseau, and Nietzsche. Subjectivism (Descartes) naturally begets sentimentalism (Rousseau), from which totalitarianism, just as naturally, emerges, managed by a group of "supermen" (Nietzsche).

Subjectivism engenders contempt for reason, which is replaced by emotions manipulated by a caste of individuals thirsty for power. The existential void caused by the castration of reason is filled by a religion of sentiment, whose new inquisitors subjugate entire peoples by "canceling" the individuals they consider inadequate. This is how the culture of tolerance morphs into the "cancel culture."

Subjectivism can only lead to totalitarianism, because it destroys all reference points. With subjectivism, everything becomes possible, even the unimaginable. Everything becomes justifiable, even the most horrendous crimes. There is no more reason, no more "common sense." There is only *my* sensitivity and those who maintain and manipulate it.

If Descartes had only known what his *cogito*—"I think"—would lead to!

Part 2 of this book will consider *the builders*: Pascal, Kierkegaard, Dostoyevsky, and Soloviev. The builders are integral personalities: their hearts, their reasons, and their wills function harmoniously, which allows them to grasp all the subjectivity of destructive thinking and to indicate ways to overcome it.

Pascal invites us *to find our hearts* in order to re-establish our reason in a world plunged into the most total subjectivity and the most abominable sentimentality.

Kierkegaard invites us *to live an authentic, unique, singular, and unrepeatable life* in a world engulfed by mass culture, conformism, political correctness, depersonalization, facelessness, and the totalitarian diktat of the so-called "general" will.

Dostoyevsky invites us *to save our humanity, our dignity, and our freedom* in a world that demands we trade them in for comfort and security.

Soloviev invites us *to practice unity of life,* to deify all aspects (personal and social) of human existence, to sanctify professional, social, and family life by imbuing it with Christian spirit, to build the kingdom of God at the very heart of society, a realm that Christians tend to shun in the name of a misunderstood humility.

These four thinkers are surprisingly topical. Each in his own way and with his own charisma enlightens us, inspires us, and incites us to action.

Part 1

THE DESTROYERS

1

THE RATIONALISM OF RENÉ DESCARTES
(1596–1650)

RENÉ DESCARTES WAS BORN on March 31, 1596, in La Haye-en-Touraine, between Tours and Poitiers, France, into a family of minor nobility. He was the youngest of the family's three sons.

His mother died when he was only one year old.

His father, who was a counselor at the Parliament of Brittany in the city of Rennes, rarely saw his children. René's maternal grandmother took charge of his education.

As a child, René was distinguished by his incredible curiosity. His father called him "my little philosopher." He did his primary and secondary studies at the prestigious Jesuit college of La Flèche, near Angers.

As the child's health was clearly precarious, the Jesuits allowed him to get up in the morning at eleven o'clock rather than five o'clock like the other students. Descartes remained faithful to this custom for the rest of his life.

At the age of twenty he finished his schooling, deeply disgusted by the education he had received. He wrote:

> As soon as I had finished the entire course of study, at the close of which it is customary to be admitted into the order of the learned, I completely changed my opinion. For I found myself involved in so many doubts and errors, that I was convinced I had advanced no farther in all my attempts at learning, than the discovery at every turn of my own ignorance. And yet I was studying in one of the most celebrated schools in Europe, in which I thought there must be learned men, if such were anywhere to be found.[1]

He continued:

> For these reasons, as soon as my age permitted me to pass from under the control of my instructors, I entirely abandoned the study of letters, and resolved no longer to seek any other science than the knowledge I could find within me, or in the great book of the world. I spent the remainder of my youth in traveling, in visiting courts and armies, in holding intercourse with men of different dispositions and ranks, in collecting varied experience, in proving myself in the different situations into which fortune threw me, and, above all, in making such reflection on the matter of my experience as to secure any benefit from it."[2]

After studying law for some time in Poitiers, at the age of twenty-two he joined the army: first in Holland, a Protestant country but an ally of France in the war

---

1. R. Descartes, *Discourse on Method*, part 1.
2. Descartes, *Discourse on Method*, part 1.

against Spain, then in Germany, in the Catholic League at war against the Czech Protestants.

In Holland he met Isaac Beeckman, known for his mathematical analysis of physical phenomena. In Germany he became interested in the Rosicrucians, who espoused esoteric principles, and to whom he dedicated his book *The Mathematical Thesaurus of Polybius, the Cosmopolitan* (1619).

On November 10, 1619, in Bavaria, Descartes, freezing in the early morning cold, took refuge in a wall-mounted stove and spent the rest of the day inside of it, thinking. He suddenly had a vision of a mathematical representation of the universe whose laws could be deduced by means of certain universal mathematical formulas. "On November 10, 1619," we read in his diary, "filled with enthusiasm, I found the foundation of an admirable science,"[3] one that allows the building of any kind of knowledge on the solid foundation of mathematics.

Deeply moved by his discovery, Descartes went into a trance. On the night of November 10, he had three successive dreams which convinced him that he had found favor with God. He vowed to go on pilgrimage to the shrine of Our Lady of Loreto "before the end of November" to give thanks to God for having inspired his discovery of "the new science."

He did not fulfill his vow. He did not go to Loreto until four years later, during a trip to Italy that he made for very different reasons.

---

3. R. Descartes, *Olympica*, fragment.

He wrote:

> I thought it necessary first of all to endeavor to establish [the principles of the new science]. And because I observed, besides, that an inquiry of this kind was of all others of the greatest moment, and one in which precipitancy and anticipation in judgment were most to be dreaded, I thought that I ought not to approach it till I had reached a more mature age (being at that time but twenty-three), and had first of all employed much of my time in preparation for the work, as well by eradicating from my mind all the erroneous opinions I had up to that moment accepted, as by amassing variety of experience to afford materials for my reasonings, and by continually exercising myself in my chosen method with a view to increased skill in its application.[4]

Descartes left the army in 1621 and spent some time in Italy. In 1625, he moved to Paris, where his scientific work led to his discovery of the principle of virtual velocities. In 1628, he joined Richelieu's army, which laid siege to the city of La Rochelle, a Huguenot stronghold.

In 1629, seeking calm and security (he feared persecution for his ideas by the French state), he moved back to Holland (Protestant and republican) where he undertook a large epistolary correspondence with the most famous scientists of the time. He studied the most diverse sciences, from medicine to meteorology. During his twenty years in Holland, he changed his residence

---

4. Descartes, *Discourse on Method*, part 2.

fifteen times, without ever revealing his address to his correspondents.

In 1634, he completed his *Treatise on Light*, but when he learned that the Inquisition had just condemned Galileo for his assertions concerning the movement of Earth, he became frightened (Descartes, like Galileo, was a supporter of heliocentrism) and decided not to publish his work.

In 1635, Francine, Descartes' natural daughter, was born. She died of scarlet fever at the age of five. For René, this was a terrible shock.

In 1637, he published *Discourse on Method*, in which he stated the thesis "I think, therefore I am," and in 1641, *Meditations on First Philosophy*, in which he expounded his doctrine on the dualism of the soul and the body (the soul and the body, according to Descartes, are two separate and independent substances). In 1644, he published his *Principles of Philosophy*, in which he asserted that the universe, although created by God, functions as an autonomous organism.

The *Meditations* and the *Principles* did not sell well. Descartes' popularity did not come from his books, but from a relatively small group of admirers who propagated his ideas.

Holland turned out not to be the bastion of freedom he had thought it was: Protestant fanatics accused him of atheism.

Descartes entered into correspondence with Queen Christina of Sweden through his friend Pierre Chanut, France's ambassador to that country. A bold and erudite woman, Christina invited him to her court and in

September 1649 sent a Swedish warship to fetch him to Stockholm.

Christina asked Descartes to give her lessons—every morning at five o'clock! For Descartes, who had been accustomed to getting up late since childhood, rising so early proved a cruel mortification that weakened his health. He caught a chill. It turned into pneumonia, from which he died on February 11, 1650.

Initially, the Jesuits considered his philosophy a useful instrument in the struggle against materialist thought which was flourishing at the time, but later perceived the danger it posed to the Christian faith and declared war on it. Louis XIV forbade the teaching of Descartes' philosophy in all French schools. However, the popularity and influence of the scholar-philosopher only increased. In the last years of the seventeenth century, when the official attacks against Descartes ceased, it became necessary to face the facts: in the universities of France, it was no longer the realistic philosophy of Aristotle that was taught, but the rationalist philosophy of Descartes.

Seventeen years after the philosopher's death, his remains were transferred from Stockholm to Paris, where they came to rest in the Church of Saint-Germain-des-Prés. Although the French Revolutionary parliament planned to transfer Descartes' ashes to the Pantheon in 1792, they remain to this day at Saint-Germain-des-Prés. His skull experienced a special fate: it was put on permanent display at the National Museum of Natural History.

Descartes was the founder of all the theoretical natural sciences of modern times, although in the field of experimental physics he was surpassed by Pascal. He was a genius of analysis, even if he sometimes made questionable assertions. He believed, for example, that the human soul is located in the pineal gland.

With his thesis "I think, therefore I am," Descartes laid the foundations of modern philosophy, becoming, unwittingly, the intellectual father of subjectivism, agnosticism, and contemporary atheism.

Descartes' Personality

Descartes was dry and egotistical. Although he had many admirers, it seems that he loved no one.

Although all his life he claimed to be a faithful son of the Catholic Church, in reality he was indifferent to religion. He went to Mass on Sundays and did his best to avoid being accused of heresy, but his Catholicism was only a formality, a calculation to please those around him. Shy and cautious, he sought to avoid trouble with the civil authorities and the clergy.

When a group of Catholic scholars, undeterred by Galileo's condemnation, intervened to defend Copernicus' heliocentric teaching, Descartes remained silent. He showed little evidence of sincerity or transparency. His motto was, *Qui bene latuit, bene vixit*—"He lives well who lays well hidden."

Descartes believed, it seems, in the "basic" truths of the Christian religion: the existence of God, the Creation of the world, the immortality of the soul, the free will of man, the Incarnation. But the only thing we can be certain about is that he was trying to convince us of the compatibility of his thinking with these truths. And the more he insisted, the more dubious his orthodoxy appeared.

Descartes did not distinguish himself by his military virtues. In Holland and Germany, he did not make war: he did mathematics. The army was for him only a way to travel. He went to La Rochelle not to fight but to contemplate the remarkable engineering works related to the siege.

Descartes' self-esteem was beyond measure. He was convinced that he was being criticized out of jealousy. He claimed that he did not borrow anything from other scholars. He refused to recognize their merits. Their reputation and glory mortified him.

One example was a trip to France in 1645, during which he met Pascal. The two scientists discussed the question of Torricelli's barometer. In 1648, Pascal carried out his famous experiment at the Puy de Dôme volcano in France's Massif Central to test the hypothesis of the "weight of the earth's atmosphere." Descartes, who could not stand the idea that a major experiment could be conducted without his participation, would later say that he himself had inspired Pascal. Pascal denied this: he said the need to perform the experiment was so obvious that he did not need Descartes to tell him so.

Descartes' moral philosophy is limited to a few simple, unoriginal rules:

> The first was to obey the laws and customs of my country, adhering firmly to the faith in which, by the

grace of God, I had been educated from my childhood and regulating my conduct in every other matter according to the most moderate opinions, and the farthest removed from extremes, which should happen to be adopted in practice with general consent of the most judicious of those among whom I might be living. . . . My second maxim was to be as firm and resolute in my actions as I was able. . . . My third maxim was to endeavor always to overcome myself rather than acquire a fortune and to change my desires rather than the order of the world.[5]

If the second rule (to resolutely carry out one's decisions) is a call to practice virtue, the first (do not fall into "excess") and the third (do not undertake to improve society) are a call to pusillanimity. Even today, they leave the scholar's admirers perplexed.

Descartes' mind was powerful, but his heart and will were dysfunctional. His moral sense, like his religious sense, showed signs of advanced atrophy.

The Only Certainty Is Mathematical

Luther, who believed himself to be a sinner, suffered from being uncertain he would be saved. So he created a system which eliminated all doubt: *I am saved if I believe that Jesus Christ is my Savior. My sins hardly matter—neither their number, nor their nature.*

---

5. Descartes, *Discourse on Method*, part 3.

Descartes also wanted to be certain. It was not religious certainties he sought concerning the salvation of his soul, but intellectual certainties stemming from knowledge. Neither theological, metaphysical, nor intuitive certainties, but *mathematical* certainties! For Descartes, certainty can only be *mathematical*. "I was especially delighted," he wrote, "with the mathematics, on account of the certitude and evidence of their reasonings."[6]

The desire for certainty in the field of knowledge is reasonable (we cannot believe just anything), but the desire for exclusively *mathematical* certainty is insane. Man knows first with his heart, then with his reason. "The faculty that allows us to grasp first principles is the heart," says Pascal. "Knowledge of first principles, like space, time, motion, number, is as solid as any derived through reason. . . . Principles are intuited, propositions are inferred, and all with certainty, though by different means."[7]

Descartes doubted the reality of first principles. For him, the heart is useless as an instrument of knowledge. Knowledge can only be mathematical. He believed that a science not based on mathematics is no science at all.

According to him, we know the truth by the method of "clear and distinct" ideas. These are *mathematically evident* ideas. They are the building blocks of science. All other ideas must be reduced to these or excluded. The

---

6. Descartes, *Discourse on Method*, part 1.

7. B. Pascal, *Pensées* (1670), section 4, "Of the Means of Belief," no. 284.

world is transparent to our gaze because it is only a geometrical extension entirely subject to our intelligence.

The Mind and the Body: Two Independent Substances

Descartes was convinced that the soul and the body are two substances absolutely *independent* of each other, whereas the philosophy of the Middle Ages proclaimed the substantial unity of the human organism: the human being is made up of a material body and a spiritual soul which together form the same, unique substance.

According to Descartes, the human soul knows the world not through the body (the senses), but innately. Descartes reconstructed the human intelligence according to the angelic model. Angels, who are pure spirits, perceive reality by means of ideas received from God at the very moment of their creation. These innate ideas allow them to know created things without intermediary, in the very light of the act by which they were created. They do not reason: they see. Descartes' "clear and distinct ideas," like those of angels, do not come from the material world but from God. For the French philosopher, human intellect, like that of the angels, does not reason, but sees reality, embraces it directly.

According to Descartes the soul does not need the body. And the body does not need the soul. The body is a machine that propels itself.

Descartes overestimated the capacities of the human soul and underestimated the dignity of the human body. Man is not an angel: he knows through the senses! The human body is not a machine: it is vivified by a spiritual soul!

The Cartesian man is not a man: he is an angel or a machine depending on how you look at him. Descartes is the founder of modern idealism as well as materialism.

Our Senses Deceive Us

According to Descartes, the most common mistake is to assume that my ideas, or perceptions, come from things. It seems reasonable to suppose that something foreign to myself imprints its image on me. But *does* it? I tend to believe that it does, but this is only a belief, not a proof. "The senses often deceive us," Descartes said. Knowledge must come from reason and not from the senses!

In reality, man cannot know except by his reason and his senses combined. Only the angelic intelligence can know without the participation of the senses.

On this level of knowledge Kant will push Descartes' work to its extreme. He will say, roughly, to the French philosopher: "You are right, René, when you say that the senses are useless for knowledge, but you are wrong when you claim that man knows things innately. The thinking intellect knows only the thought itself or its representations, but the thing behind these representations—the thing in itself—is unknowable."

Descartes closed the traditional way of knowledge and opened a new one. But this one turned out to be wrong. Descartes' "methodic doubt" ("I doubt methodically in order to know reality") becomes total agnosticism with Kant ("I know only my thought; I do not have access to being, and reality is unknowable") and absolute idealism with Hegel ("My thought, this is being; it is useless to look for it elsewhere, for my thought produces the reality!").

I Think, Therefore I Am

My body, says Descartes, is perhaps illusory. My thought, on the other hand, can only be real:

> As I observed that this truth—*I think, therefore I am*—was so certain and of such evidence that no ground of doubt, however extravagant, could be alleged by the skeptics capable of shaking it, I concluded that I might, without scruple, accept it as the first principle of the philosophy of which I was in search.[8]

My existence, Descartes insists, is proven by the fact that I think. If I stopped thinking, the evidence of my existence would disappear. Therefore, I exist when I think, and only when I think.

Descartes makes *being* directly dependent on *thinking*. If, formerly, our capacity to think was considered a consequence of our being ("I think because I am"), now our being becomes a consequence of our capacity to think ("I am because I think"). According to Kant, Descartes realized a "Copernican revolution" in philosophy: it is no longer God who is the center, but the thinking subject.

---

8. Descartes, *Discourse on Method*, part 4.

In making *cogito*—"I think"—philosophy's point of departure, Descartes set in motion a process whereby transcendent realities (God, being, the good, the beautiful) are transformed into "by-products" of thought. By his thought, man produces God, who remains in his thought. This God is man himself!

By placing the thinking subject at the center, Descartes suppresses God, because a peripheral god is not God but a product of our thinking. To Descartes' formula *Cogito, ergo sum*, we should oppose Franz von Baader's *Cogitor, ergo sum*—"I am thought, therefore I am." In other words, God thought of me from all eternity, and that is why he created me. And if I continue to exist, it is because God does not cease to think of me and to give me being. If he were to stop doing so for even a single second, I would instantly turn into nothingness. For Baader, a German philosopher of the late eighteenth and early nineteenth centuries, God is the center, while man—the thinking subject—is the periphery. Such is the rational order of things.

At the time of Descartes, the philosophy of Greek antiquity and the European Middle Ages needed to be remodeled, but with Descartes it was simply swept away. Before Descartes, we sought to understand the place God had assigned us in the universe; after Descartes, we asserted that we "create" our own universe within ourselves. Descartes is at the philosophical origin of a vision of the world in which the thinking subject is the source and the center of all things.

LIVING ACCORDING TO DESCARTES

Descartes created a new type of man: the rationalist.

For the rationalist, the great question of existence is that of knowledge: "What can I know with certainty?" By certainty he means "mathematical certainty."

The rationalist is an exclusively intellectual being. He is incapable of a sensory, heartfelt, and joyful exchange with the object of knowledge, of an authentic encounter with it. He coldly analyzes reality but does not "commune" with it. His knowledge does not touch him, does not affect him in the depths of his interior self. Tending to be emotionally inexpressive, he can respond to what he knows neither with joy, nor sadness, nor compassion, nor love. His senses atrophy.

Intellectual analysis is the goal! But the distance he keeps from the object of his analysis is so great that he is unable to penetrate and contemplate it, and therefore to know it.

The rationalist reduces all reality to his poor ability to understand it. Outwardly, he looks intelligent, but his understanding of things is extremely limited—like a computer.

2

JEAN-JACQUES ROUSSEAU'S SENTIMENTALISM
(1712–1778)

ROUSSEAU WAS BORN on June 28, 1712, in Geneva, Switzerland, the seat of Calvinism since 1536.

After his father, a watchmaker, quarreled with a compatriot, the family fled to a neighboring canton.

His mother died of a postpartum infection a week after his birth. In women, and especially in his mistresses, Rousseau would seek a mother for the rest of his life.

From the age of ten, Jean-Jacques lived in Geneva under the care of his maternal uncle. He spent two years in a Calvinist boarding school, was then entrusted to a notary, and then to an engraver who treated him severely. One day, fearing that he would be punished for coming home late, he decided to run away. He was fifteen years old.

Beyond the gates of Geneva lies Catholic Savoy. There, a destitute Rousseau asked a priest to help him. The priest sent him to a certain Madame de Warens, an affluent twenty-nine-year-old baroness who had been born into a Swiss Protestant family, recently left her husband, and settled in Annecy, Savoy, where she embraced Catholicism.

Françoise-Louise de Warens arranged for Rousseau to take up residence in the *Hospice des catéchumènes* in Turin, Italy, a training center for catechumens. Nine days later, Rousseau became a Catholic.

In Turin, he began working as a secretary and virtual lackey for a noble lady, who died three months later. After her death, Jean-Jacques was found to be in possession of a costly object—a ribbon—that he had stolen from the deceased. He claimed that the ribbon was given to him by a girl, a young cook in the employ of the old lady. The household believed him and punished the girl. "When I accused the unhappy girl, it is strange, but strictly true, that my friendship for her was the immediate cause of it. She was present to my thoughts; I formed my excuse from the first object that presented itself."[1]

In 1729, Rousseau returned to Madame de Warens. He was seventeen years old; she was thirty. She became his guide and mistress. He called her "mother," usually "mommy." She taught him to write well and to express himself in the language of educated people.

Concerned about the future of her pupil, Madame de Warens sent him to the seminary, then to apprentice with an organist, but he soon gave up the organ. Rousseau returned to Annecy. In the meantime, Madame de Warens had already left for Paris.

---

1. J.-J. Rousseau, *Confessions* (1782), part 1, bk. 2.

For more than two years, Rousseau wandered about Switzerland. In the spring of 1732, he again became the guest of Madame de Warens, who was living with a certain Claude Anet, a young Swiss convert who was also her gardener's nephew. They set up house as a *ménage à trois*.

On Anet's death at the age of twenty-eight, which Rousseau attributed to pneumonia, he found himself alone with Madame de Warens. The baroness sent him to Montpellier to be treated for his heart tumor. During this trip, he met Madame de Larnage. She had ten children and was twenty years his senior (she was forty-five, he was twenty-five). For three days, they lived together: "Oh! These three days! What reason have I to regret them! Never did such happiness return again."[2]

When he returned, he found the baroness with a new lover, once again a young Swiss man who had just converted. Rousseau called him "brother." A new *ménage à trois* was established.

It was then that the first signs of Rousseau's misanthropy began to appear. He often isolated himself. He sought solace in nature: he arose at dawn, worked in the garden, and took up beekeeping.

In 1740, at the age of twenty-eight, he got a job as a tutor in a family in Lyon but quickly resigned because he did not know how to behave with children or adults. He then obtained the position of private secretary to the French ambassador in Venice. He made himself important, imagining himself to be a diplomat. The

---

2. Rousseau, *Confessions*, part 1, bk. 6.

ambassador, appalled, sent him away without even paying him his salary.

In Paris, Rousseau had an affair with a waitress of the hotel where he was staying—Marie-Thérèse Levasseur, a young, illiterate, peasant girl. He said that he had never felt the slightest love for her, but this did not prevent him from marrying her civilly twenty years later. Together they had five children, whom Rousseau placed in the *Enfants-Trouvés*, a home for abandoned children. "This arrangement seemed to me so good, reasonable and lawful, that if I did not publicly boast of it, it was merely out of consideration for the mother."[3] He felt this showed him to be a true father and a good citizen.

After obtaining a position as a secretary to a merchant, Rousseau began to frequent the circle to which the famous Madame d'Épinay and Denis Diderot, the leader of the French Encyclopedists, belonged.

In 1749, at the age of thirty-seven, Rousseau visited Diderot, who was imprisoned in the chateau at Vincennes. On the way, he read in the *Mercure de France* that the Academy of Dijon had established a competition to answer the question: "Has the restoration of the sciences and arts contributed to the purification of morals?"

In a letter to his friend, Chrétien-Guillaume de Malesherbes, Rousseau recounts in detail the impact the announcement of the *Mercure de France* competition had on him:

---

3. Rousseau, *Confessions,* part 2, bk. 8.

> If anything ever resembled a flash of inspiration, it is the turmoil that took place within me upon reading that announcement. Suddenly I feel my spirit dazzled by a thousand brilliant insights. A host of ideas crowd in upon me all at once, troubling my mind with a force and confusion impossible to express. I feel my head spinning with a giddiness like intoxication. A violent palpitation oppresses and expands my breast, finding it no longer possible to breathe while walking, I let myself collapse beneath one of the trees which line the avenue; there I spend half an hour in such a state of agitation that on rising I discover the front of my vest to be wet with tears I never knew I had shed. Oh Sir, had I ever been able to write one quarter of what I saw and felt beneath that tree, how clearly I would have revealed all the contradictions of the social system; how forcefully I would have exposed all the abuses of our institutions; how simply I would have demonstrated that man is naturally good, and that it is only through these institutions that he becomes evil![4]

Man is naturally good! It was an unconscious reaction to the Calvinism of his childhood, which proclaimed the *total corruption,* the *absolute depravity* of human nature caused by original sin. Man is good by nature! The sciences, the arts, and social institutions can only corrupt him!

---

4. J.-J.Rousseau, Letter to M. de Malesherbes, January 12, 1762.

For his *Discourse on the Arts and Sciences*, Rousseau won first prize. Thus, enlightened society rewarded its own detractor. Voltaire was enraged.

For Rousseau, a decade of intense activity and triumph began. Socially prominent ladies called on him. He accepted an invitation to visit his hometown. He returned to his Calvinist faith (which seems incredible after the "enlightenment" of Vincennes) and became a citizen of Geneva.

In 1754, the Academy of Dijon announced a new competition on the question "What is the origin of inequality among men, and is it authorized by the natural law?" In 1755, Rousseau wrote his second discourse, entitled *Discourse on the Origin and Basis of Inequality Among Men*. He dedicated it to the Republic of Geneva. If, in his first discourse, he denounced the sciences and the arts for their corrupting influence, in this new discourse he condemned everything that constitutes the foundation of civil life: property, the state, laws. For the first time, he publicly denied the doctrine of original sin.

Enlightened society again rapturously welcomed the condemnation being hurled at it. Madame d'Épinay has a cottage built for Rousseau on the grounds of her country estate near Saint-Denis. In the spring of 1756, he moved into his "Hermitage." Nightingales sang under his windows, and the forest became his "workroom," allowing him to wander for days in solitary contemplation.

Rousseau, aged forty-four, fell passionately in love with Madame d'Épinay's twenty-six-year-old sister-in-law, Countess Sophie d'Houdetot, who had been in love for several years with the poet Jean-François de Saint-Lambert, who was serving in the army. Rousseau, besotted, wept tears of joy at the feet of the countess, reproaching himself at the same time for betraying Saint-Lambert. Sophie, still in love with Saint-Lambert, begged Jean-Jacques to be content with a platonic friendship. In an altered and idealized form, this story come to serve as the subject of the novel *Julie, or the New Heloise*, which Rousseau publishes a few years after the incident.

Madame d'Épinay ridiculed Rousseau's love for the Countess d'Houdetot. Saint-Lambert, informed of the affair by an anonymous letter, requested a period of leave from the army. Rousseau suspected Madame d'Épinay of having betrayed him and sent her an insulting letter; she forgave him.

The contretemps with d'Épinay was soon followed by a total break with the *philosophes* and the circle of Encyclopedists. Madame d'Épinay, on her way to Geneva for a meeting with a famous doctor, asked Rousseau to accompany her. He refused. Diderot insisted that Rousseau make the trip and reproached him for his ingratitude. Rousseau was convinced that Madame d'Épinay and Diderot were trying to disgrace him by making him look like her lackey.

Rousseau took refuge with the Duke of Luxembourg, owner of the chateau of Montmorency, north of Paris. The duke put a pavilion in his park at Rousseau's disposal. Jean-Jacques spent four years there and wrote both *The New Heloise* and *Emile*. He did not hesitate to declaim his works to his hosts, although he suspected them of hypocrisy. He insulted them and declared his contempt for their social status.

In 1761, he published *The New Heloise*, in the spring of the following year *Emile*, and a few weeks later *The Social Contract*.

Julie, or The New Heloise is a novel about the impossible love of a tutor of humble origin for a young noblewoman, his pupil. This epistolary novel was a success unsurpassed in the eighteenth century by any other work of French literature. Heloise is a new literary type: a "beautiful soul," virtuous by nature, untainted by sin and in no need of God's grace. She has a pure heart: always and everywhere, she is guided by her feelings alone. She needs neither reason nor will.

Emile is a treatise on education according to "natural" principles. It was considered offensive by civil and ecclesiastical authorities as it contained the "Profession of Faith of a Savoyard Vicar" establishing the principles of natural religion as Rousseau understood them, and it antagonized both Catholics and Protestants: he expounds his "religion of the heart," criticizes the atheism and materialism of the Encyclopedists, and openly attacks the Church.

The Parliament of Paris ordered *Emile* to be burned and its author imprisoned. Fearing torture and burning at the stake, Rousseau fled to Geneva. At the Swiss border, he rushed to kiss the ground of the "country of justice and freedom." But the government of Geneva ordered the burning of both *Emile* and *The Social Contract*!

Rousseau found refuge in the Duchy of Neuchâtel, a possession of the king of Prussia, and settled in a village called Môtiers. Voltaire published an anonymous pamphlet accusing him of intending to overthrow the Geneva constitution and Christianity, and of arranging for the murder of his own mother-in-law. Indignant, the inhabitants of Môtiers decided to kill him. Rousseau fled to England, where he took refuge in the home of the philosopher David Hume.

Rousseau's nerves were badly shaken. His distrust and fearful imagination verged on mania. In just a few days, he came to see Hume as a double-crosser who had insidiously lured him to England to make him a laughingstock. Hume retaliated by revealing Rousseau's vices to English and European public opinion. Voltaire, meanwhile, gleefully urged the English to confine Rousseau to a lunatic asylum.

Rousseau returned to Paris. Despite the legal sanctions against him, no one bothered him. Alarmed by a pamphlet published in 1765 which ruthlessly exposed his past, he wrote his *Confessions* to clear his name and sincerely atone. Pride, however, took over, and his *Confessions* turned into a defense for his past behavior; few are the passages unfavorable to him, and many the ones that castigate his enemies. *Confessions* is a novel composed of two parts. The first is a poetic idyll, the outpouring of a soul in love with nature, and an idealized expression of his love for Madame de Warens. The second is imbued with malice and suspicion; not even his wife and best friends are spared.

In the spring of 1778, the Marquis de Girardin took Rousseau to his country residence at Ermenonville. At the end of June, a concert was organized in his honor on an island in the middle of the park. Rousseau expressed his wish to be buried there. A few days later, on July 2, 1778, he expired in the arms of Marie-Thérèse.

In 1789, the French Revolution broke out. In 1794, under the Convention (the revolutionary regime), the remains of Jean-Jacques Rousseau were entombed in the Pantheon, formerly a church consecrated to Saint Geneviève, the patron saint of Paris, then converted to a secular state mausoleum for the remains of distinguished French citizens. There they laid him next to the remains of his archrival Voltaire, which had been there since 1791. Both occupy places of honor near the main entrance to the building.

Rousseau's Personality

As a writer, Rousseau was talented; as a man, his defects were glaringly obvious:

- Self-sufficiency. Jean-Jacques took a religious delight in himself. His capacity for admiring himself was boundless.
- Vanity. He constantly referred to his talent, to the dignity of his writings, to his worldwide fame. "I am not made like any one I have ever known, I dare say, like no one else in existence."[5]

---

5. Rousseau, *Confessions,* part 1, bk. 1.

- Sensual voraciousness.
- Ingratitude. He quickly forgot the favors people had done for him.
- Susceptibility and distrust. He easily turned his back on the people closest to him.
- Misanthropy. He did not know how to live in society. He felt like a stranger wherever he went. He aspired to a solitude in which he was surrounded by the imaginary creatures of his dreams.

Sentimentalism: The "Religion of Emotions"

The central theme of the life of Descartes is knowledge; for Rousseau it is the emotions. Descartes wanted to *know*. Rousseau wanted to *feel*.

The point of departure for Descartes' philosophy is the *thinking* subject. For Rousseau's, it is the *feeling* subject.

For Descartes, I *am* my thinking. In Rousseau's thought, I *am* my feelings.

Rousseau makes a cult of his emotions and regards them with tenderness. His emotions are his religion. "I long for the moment when I . . . only need myself to be happy."[6] Happiness consists in being "sufficient to oneself like God."[7] I am my own happiness.

Descartes is the father of rationalism; Rousseau is the father of sentimentalism.

---

6. J.-J. Rousseau, *Emile* (1762), 1, 4.

7. Rousseau, *Reveries of the Solitary Walker*, fifth walk.

In Rousseau's personality, the heart subsumes reason and the will. "A state of reflection is a state contrary to nature," he wrote. "A thinking man is a depraved animal."[8] The "beautiful soul" is guided only by the heart. To live according to your conscience is to live according to your heart! What I feel is my conscience! Do what your heart tells you—even if it is to steal, lie, or fornicate—and you will always be right. The heart is infallible! When Rousseau stole the precious ribbon from his mistress and accused a domestic servant of theft, his conscience was clear: I am a thief, but I have a good heart! In putting his five children on the public dole, he was convinced he was acting virtuously, since it was a decision of his heart. Diderot, a materialist and atheist, had well understood the folly and the danger of such a mindset when he said to Rousseau, "I know well that, whatever you do, you will always have the testimony of your conscience on your side."[9] For Rousseau, reason and will are not attributes of morality. By *conscience* he means heart, and by *virtue* he means natural passion.

The heart of the sentimentalist—Rousseau's heart—is not a heart at all. It is a useless rag flapping in the wind. If Rousseau's personality and behavior are so contradictory, it is because without reason and without will there is neither consistency nor stability. Indeed, Jean-Jacques' life is made up of a series of antitheses:

---

8. J.-J. Rousseau, *Discourse on Inequality* (1755), first part.

9. S. M. Girardin, *Jean-Jacques Rousseau, sa vie et ses ouvrages* (*Jean-Jacques Rousseau: His Life and Work**), vol. 4, *Revue des Deux Mondes*, 1853, pp. 865–892, translation from French.

Extreme in everything, and contradicting himself at every moment, timid and impertinent, ashamed and cynical, difficult to shake up as well as to restrain, and surpassing others once he is underway, capable of impetuosity and soon falling back into inertia, fighting and flattering his century, cursing his literary reputation and aiming only at defending and increasing it, seeking solitude and wanting to be known by the whole world, shunning attention and dejected at not receiving it, decrying the great and living with them, celebrating the delights of independence and never ceasing to accept hospitality that must be paid for in clever and witty considerations, dreaming of thatched cottages and yet living in castles, consorting with a chambermaid and loving only high-class women, preaching the joys of the family and failing in his duties as a father, covering other people's children with caresses and putting his own in a hospice, effusively praising the heavenly feeling of friendship and feeling it for no one, giving himself away and immediately withdrawing, at first expansive and cordial, then suspicious and fierce, this is Rousseau.[10]

The "Noble Savage"

Rousseau did not use the term "noble savage," but the idea of a good, innocent, or pure state of nature is central to his interpretation of human nature: "Man is

---

10. A. Chuquet, *J.-J. Rousseau* (Paris, 1893), p. 199.

naturally good. . . . There is no original perversity in the human heart. . . . The first movements of nature are always upright."[11]

Man is born pure. It is society that corrupts him. Rousseau denies the Judeo-Christian teaching on original sin, that wound which we inherit from conception in the womb and which forms in the soul a focus of resistance to God's love: pride, thirst for pleasure, thirst for riches.

Rousseau does not accept this obvious fact: man is born spiritually ill. Young children are far from being pure and virtuous. They have selfish tendencies deep within them that precede education and culture.

The philosophy that denies the disordered tendencies of human nature is called *naturalism*. For the naturalist, everything that occurs in us naturally is pure and perfect; our first reaction to external stimuli does not need to be corrected. It is always noble. Instead of analyzing, thinking, choosing, and eventually resisting the impulses of certain emotions and feelings, what is needed is "living!"

"One must be oneself." This is a phrase that Rousseau often repeated in the last years of his life. Sensitivity, above all. No point in trying to become better, to want to develop one's personality—that would be tantamount to sin for Rousseau! Culture and education impinge upon the inner world of the soul—this is sacrilege!

---

11. J.-J. Rousseau, *Lettre à C. de Beaumont* (*Letter to C. de Beaumont**), translation from French (La Pléiade, 1762), pp. 935–937.

The "noble savage" needs neither conscience nor virtue, for he has a heart. Nor does he need the grace of God, for he is born pure and healthy.

The "noble savage" needs nothing. The "noble savage" thinks, who needs a society? Although society is a fact, I don't know where it comes from. I cannot destroy it, but I can rebuild it on new foundations so that it can no longer corrupt me. It is not I who must be improved, but society! Politics is the salvation of humanity! A new, perfect society must be built! A society that respects my freedom and my individuality!

This is the whole modern ideology of "progress." Rousseau's religion is a "religion of progress." The belief is that we are saved not by the spirit (the development of character), nor by religion (the outpouring of grace), but rather by politics—by the remaking of society!

A Naturalist Parody of Christianity

Rousseau is a religious reformer. His faith is that of the "Savoyard Vicar" in *Emile*. He rejects original sin and all that flows from it: the salvation of mankind through Christ, the supernatural grace he offers us, the sacraments he instituted, the redemptive and sanctifying power of his suffering and of all suffering.

Jean-Jacques wants to create a New Jerusalem on earth, which will be the fruit not of the grace of Christ but of the power of man. He empties Christianity of its supernatural content.

The philosopher Jacques Maritain posed the question: "To laicize the Gospel, to keep the human aspirations of Christianity but to do away with Christ, is not all this the whole essence of the Revolution?"[12] Was this not the essence of the French and the Bolshevik Revolutions?

In this respect, Leo Tolstoy, with his "Christianity without Christ," is a faithful son of Jean-Jacques Rousseau. Rousseau, who died eleven years before the storming of the Bastille, and Tolstoy, who died seven years before the storming of the Winter Palace, are the great inspirers of modern revolutions.

Rousseauism is a Christian heresy. Maritain asserts,

> It is to Rousseau that we owe this corpse of Christian ideas whose immense putrefaction poisons the universe today. . . . If the world does not live by the living Christianity in the Church, it dies from the corrupted Christianity outside the Church.[13]

Rousseau laid the cornerstone for the creation of a new religion, which since the end of the nineteenth century has been called *modernism*. Modernism is an interpretation of Christianity from the point of view of Cartesian rationalism ("my religion is the product of my thinking") and Rousseauian sentimentalism ("my faith is the product of my feeling"). For modernism, there is nothing transcendent or supernatural about Christianity: it is a purely human invention.

Rousseau learned to stop believing in original sin, hell, and redemption from Madame de Warens. She

---

12. J. Maritain, *Three Reformers: Luther, Descartes, Rousseau* (Paris, 1925; London, 1928), chapter on Rousseau, p. 15.

13. Maritain, *Three Reformers*, chapter on Rousseau, p. 16.

taught him to live by the impulses of the heart and the flesh without ever feeling remorse of conscience—even while continuing to consider himself a good Christian!

> It was with Madame de Warens that Jean-Jacques developed his naturalistic religiosity. . . . Madame de Warens was not content with initiating Jean-Jacques and Claude Anet, the gardener, into the blessings of sexual communism; she initiated Jean-Jacques at the same time into the life of the spirit. . . . If Jean-Jacques is the father of modernism, Madame de Warens deserves to be called its mommy. . . . Not nearly as vile or despicable as Voltaire, Rousseau was vastly worse, because he gave men not just the means to negate religion, but a religion outside of the indivisible Truth. . . . He led modern thought toward an abominable sentimentality, an infernal parody of Christianity.[14]

For the Russian philosopher Vladimir Soloviev, "Christianity without Christ" is the most unimaginable lie and deception known to mankind and is the clearest sign of the consummation of the world and of Christ's return to earth.[15]

The Social Contract

According to Rousseau, the natural man (the "noble savage") is a solitary being. He is not called to live in society.

---

14. Maritain, *Three Reformers*, chapter on Rousseau, p. 18.
15. See V. Soloviev, *A Short Story of the Anti-Christ* (1900).

But if society exists—and its existence is an indisputable fact—then how can its existence be justified?

One cannot justify a society that enslaves the freeborn person. It is only possible to justify a society that is the result of a *social contract*, by virtue of which everyone, in obeying everyone, obeys no one in particular. For this to happen, each person must surrender his natural rights to the community—to the "General Will." He must cease to exist as an individual and now exist only as a part of the community. In doing so, to submit to the General Will is to submit to oneself and thereby to be free.

Thus, Rousseau proclaims the emergence of the social self and the abolition of the individual self. In the state of nature, we existed only as individuals; in society we exist only as parts of the whole, as insignificant fractions of it. This is how individualism (which does not recognize the reality of the social bonds imposed by nature) leads fatally to socialism, at the very moment when it sets out to build society.

The anthropology of Rousseau (the socializing individualist) is deeply flawed. Our sociability is not the result of a contract. We are social beings by nature. There is no individual state and no social state distinct from it. We are both individuals and social beings. Human rights are not contractual: we are natural and inalienable.

According to Rousseau, in submitting to a law I voted against, I remain free, because I do not vote to express my opinion but to know the General Will, which is revealed by the result of the vote. Therefore, if an opinion I was opposed to wins, it only means that I was mistaken and that what I thought was the General Will was not.

> What is he offering us here," Maritain asks, "but the absurd transposition of the case of the believer who asks in prayer for things he regards as appropriate, yet, at the same time, asks above all that God's will be done? He conceives of voting as a kind of prayer addressed to the General Will.[16]

Rousseau substitutes the General Will for the will of God and his commandments.

If someone refuses to obey the General Will, others will force him to do so; in other words, he will be "forced" to be free! This exercise in sophistry gave rise to the idea and practice of Jacobinism with fatal consequences. Rousseau not only inspired the French Revolution of 1789, but he was also its spiritual leader.

Hobbes in his *Leviathan* consciously sought to strengthen monarchical absolutism, whereas Rousseau unconsciously worked in favor of democratic totalitarianism.

After having glorified the "state of nature" and having stigmatized society and the state as being based on lies and violence, Rousseau proclaimed the "state of society," the aim of which is to castrate the individual in the name of a powerful state!

The "religion" of the *Social Contract* is just as insane as the "religion" of *Emile* and *The New Heloise*.

---

16. Maritain, *Three Reformers*, chapter on Rousseau, p. 13, 6.

LIVING ACCORDING TO ROUSSEAU

Rousseau created the modern type of the "socializing individualist": his individual self excludes society while his social self excludes his individuality.

As an individual, he has no other rule of life than his sensitivity. He is a sentimentalist. His emotions are his religion. His emotions are his conscience and his virtue. He is devoid of a sense of sin. He is devoid of reason and will. His existence is disjointed. He contradicts himself at every moment.

Socially he exists only as part of the whole. He fulfills himself in the politically and culturally correct. He belongs to the herd. Psychobabble is his daily bread. Progress is his religion.

3

FRIEDRICH NIETZSCHE'S VOLUNTARISM
(1844–1900)

NIETZSCHE WAS BORN on October 15, 1844, in Röcken, near Leipzig, in what is now Germany. His father, Carl-Ludwig, like his two grandfathers, was a Lutheran pastor.

Carl-Ludwig died at the age of thirty-five of a hereditary disease that took the form of violent migraine attacks. Friedrich was only five years old. Two years later, his younger brother, Ludwig Joseph, also died. Friedrich, his mother, and his sister Elisabeth (two years his junior) moved to Naumburg.

At the age of fourteen, Friedrich entered the Pforta Gymnasium, a boarding school for the most gifted students in Germany. He wanted to become a musician but his mother talked him out of it.

Like his father, Nietzsche suffered from insomnia and migraines. His vision was also impaired.

At the age of twenty, he began his studies in literature and theology at the University of Bonn, and continued at the University of Leipzig.

In Leipzig, he lost his faith and abandoned the study of theology. He devoted himself exclusively to Greek language and literature. Nietzsche was a philologist: his written works make use of parables, images, paradoxes, riddles, and aphorisms.

One day he stumbled into a bookshop and bought a book by Arthur Schopenhauer entitled *The World as Will and Representation*. The world is governed by a demented and terrifying will, Schopenhauer asserted. This book made a very strong impression on the young Nietzsche, whose suffering only worsened.

In 1868, he was invited to teach classical philology at the University of Basel in Switzerland. For several years, Nietzsche was close to the composer Richard Wagner, with whom he shared a passion for ancient Greece and the works of Schopenhauer.

In 1870, during the Franco-Prussian War, he enlisted as a volunteer nurse. In 1871, he returned to Basel, where he resumed his teaching activities.

In 1872, he wrote *The Birth of Tragedy*, in which he set out his vision of the dualist origins of art. In the art of ancient Greece, he saw the constant struggle between two principles, which he described as Apollonian (rational) and Dionysian (chaotic). The task of modern man he asserted, is to revive the Dionysian side of existence.

At the age of thirty, he became practically blind and began to experience serious stomach problems. Suffering from paralysis, violent nausea, blindness, and migraines, Nietzsche became cynical, gloomy, and desperate.

He spent the winter of 1876–1877 in Sorrento, Italy, but the mild Mediterranean climate did not ease his suffering. He lived in isolation in Genoa, then in the Swiss mountains, in the village of Sils-Maria.

In 1878, he wrote *Human, All Too Human*. This was the first book in which he set out his nihilistic view of life. It marked the beginning of his struggle against everything he had once held dear. In the preface, which he wrote ten years later, he asks:

> Why renounce everything that I respected, indeed, respect itself? Why this coldness, this suspicion, this hatred of my very virtues? . . . You had to become master of yourself, and of your own virtues. Before, they were *your* masters: but they have the right only to be your instruments. You had to . . . learn the art of using them or getting rid of them in the service of your higher aims.[1]

At the age of thirty-five, having gone on leave several times for ill health, he was forced to retire. He wrote to his theologian friend Franz Overbeck: "*Sum in puncto desperationis. Dolor vincit vitam voluntatemque.* [I am desperate. Pain has overwhelmed my life and my will.]"[2]

In 1882, he wrote *The Gay Science*, which contains the famous aphorism "God is dead."

In Rome, Nietzsche met Louisa Gustav von Salomé. "Lou" was a writer, philosopher, and psychoanalyst. She was born in 1861 in St. Petersburg into the family of Gustav von Salomé, a Balt of German origin and a

---

1. F. Nietzsche, *Human, All Too Human* (1878), preface, p. 6.
2. F. Nietzsche, Letter to F. Overbeck, September 18, 1881.

general in the Russian army. Lou was an "emancipated" young woman. Many prominent persons fell in love with her: she was Nietzsche's "Great Russian Revolution." The Austrian poet Rainer Maria Rilke idolized her; she was his mistress for three years when he was only twenty-one and she thirty-five. Freud admired her.

Nietzsche wanted to marry Lou. She refused; they parted ways. Instead, Lou married Friedrich Andreas, a professor of Oriental languages. It was an unusual *ménage*: Lou and Friedrich had no relations with each other, but Lou had many lovers and Friedrich impregnated the chambermaid.

In desperation because of her refusal, Nietzsche composed the first part of *Thus Spoke Zarathustra* (1883) in only ten days, in which he sets out his doctrine of the superman. Lou seems to be the prototype of his Zarathustra. She is indeed the embodiment of the Nietzschean credo: "Become what you are!" by which he really meant, "Become whatever you want!"

After *Zarathustra*, Nietzsche wrote *Beyond Good and Evil* (1886), *The Antichrist* (1888) and *Ecce Homo* (1888).

In 1885, his sister Elisabeth married Bernhard Förster, an anti-Semite, who committed suicide four years later. Nietzsche, who declared himself to be an "anti-anti-Semite," broke with his sister just as he had with the Judeophobic circle of Richard Wagner a few years earlier. For Nietzsche, anti-Semitism was the mark of a low, cowardly, and envious person of populist mentality.

Nietzsche's illness only got worse. In 1887, he wrote to Overbeck: "Ten years of illness . . . These last ten years have given me ample opportunity to understand what it means to be alone."[3]

In 1888 he went mad. Overbeck had him admitted to a psychiatric hospital in Basel, where he remained until March 1890, when his mother took him into her home in Naumburg. After his mother's death in 1897, Friedrich was unable to move or speak. His sister took care of him. He remained in that condition until his death in 1900.

He is buried in the old churchyard in Röcken, Germany.

Nietzsche's Personality

Suffering, loneliness, despair: this is the key to understanding Nietzsche.

> There were days which he spent entirely in bed. A prey to cramp in the stomach, to nausea, reduced to semi-consciousness by pain, his temples pulsing furiously, his eyes blinded by suffering. No one came near him to place a cooling bandage on his forehead, to read to him, to talk or to laugh.[4]

Nietzsche wrote to his sister: "I have neither God nor friends. . . . If only I had a small circle of friends willing to listen to me and understand me, I would be in

---

3. Nietzsche, Letter to F. Overbeck, November 12, 1887.

4. S. Zweig, *Friedrich Nietzsche* (1925), quoted in "'Nietzche's Seventh Solitude,' by Stefan Zweig," Anthologia, May 23, 2021, accessed August 4, 2023, https://www.anthologialitt.com/post/stefanzweig-nietzsche-sseventhsolitude.

perfect health."[5] In his *Zarathustra* he complains: "They all speak of me when they sit around their fire in the evening—they speak of me, but no one thinks of me!"[6]

Instead of sanctifying pain through the Christian faith (which he lost) or trying to free himself from it through nirvana, like Schopenhauer, Nietzsche hid his suffering under the mask of cruelty. The identification of pain with life in his writing is his way of hiding his own vulnerability. Nietzsche is the symbol of the suffering man who hides his despair. His cruelty is a mask. "Every profound spirit needs a mask,"[7] says Nietzsche. "I am *one* thing; my creations are another."[8]

"I shudder at the thought of all the unjust and inadequate who, one day or another, will claim my authority."[9] Nietzsche will have done everything to ensure that this "injustice" and this "inadequacy" occur.

Life as Chaos

In 1872, Nietzsche, at the age of twenty-eight, wrote *The Birth of Tragedy from the Spirit of Music*, in which he put forward two principles that he believed to be the basis of culture: the Dionysian principle and the Apollonian principle.

---

5. F. Nietzsche, Letter to E. Förster-Nietzsche, July 8, 1886.

6. F. Nietzsche, *Thus Spoke Zarathustra* (1883), part 3, chap. 49, "The Bedwarfing Virtue", p. 2.

7. F. Nietzsche, *Beyond Good and Evil* (1886), part 2, aphorism 40.

8. F. Nietzsche, *Ecce Homo* (1908), "Why I Write Such Excellent Books," p. 1.

9. F. Nietzsche, Letter to Malwida von Meysenbug, June 1884.

In Greek mythology, Dionysus is the god of wine and the productive forces of nature; Apollo is the god of light. For Nietzsche, the Dionysian spirit embodies the lust for life: it is an anarchic, uncontrolled, and intoxicating passion that emanates from the depths of nature. The Apollonian principle is its opposite: it represents form, order, harmony, limits, and measure.

The Apollonian opposes the Dionysian element as the *artificial* opposes the *natural*, repressing all that is excessive and disproportionate. These two principles are, however, inseparable. They struggle against each other in the artist's heart but coexist in his work.

In the Dionysian orgy there are no individuals, there is only a shapeless mass of intoxicated bodies. The Apollonian principle is, on the contrary, a principle of individuation.

In the great tragedies of the playwright Aeschylus (525–456 BC) (*Prometheus, Agamemnon*), these two principles combine harmoniously. This is the world of ideal art where the chaotic Dionysian will is expressed through Apollonian imagery. In Nietzsche's eyes, this is the most beautiful period in the history of art.

With Sophocles (495–406) (*Antigone, Ajax, Electra*) the process of the degradation of tragedy begins, asserts Nietzsche. Sophocles thinks and overthinks!

With Euripides (480–406) (*Medea, The Trojans, Iphigenia*) we witness the death of tragedy. Euripides is a man of reason. Everything is clear to him; the motivation of his characters is transparent. For Nietzsche, reason is synonymous with mediocrity.

Nietzsche breaks with the German aesthetic tradition which finds ancient Greece optimistic, luminous, rational. He is the first to speak of another Greece: the tragic, chaotic, voluntaristic Greece.

For Nietzsche, the classical Greece we know and love—that of Socrates, Plato, and Aristotle—is not the real Greece. It is a decadent Greece. The real Greece he asserts, is the pre-classical, pre-Socratic Greece, the Greece of Attic tragedy, of competition and war. The *Iliad* is an aristocratic work! Aristocracy and competition, for Nietzsche, are one and the same thing.

In Nietzsche's world, Socrates does not love life; he is a criminal who claims to "correct" life by the "dictatorship of reason"! As soon as Socrates enters the scene, as soon as rationality is imposed, instinct disappears! Socrates expelled Dionysus from culture and made Apollo the symbol of a worthless and unbearable rationality! This is the cause of the crisis of philosophy and culture!

Dionysus becomes Nietzsche's universal rule, the perfect measure, the sole criterion of judgment. He will never abandon this principle.

Nietzsche renounces the Logos, Reason, Wisdom. What counts for him is Instinct, Will, Power. He identifies Life with Chaotic Power. "In the beginning was the Word," writes the apostle John. "In the beginning was the Will," Nietzsche tells us, following Schopenhauer. An irrational and uncontrollable Will.

He posits that after Plato—and this is frightening!—life acquires a meaning, a transcendent goal. Christianity confirms and reinforces rationality. Nietzsche renounces all metaphysics, both Plato's and Christianity's, "because Christianity is Platonism for the 'people.'"[10] For Nietzsche, reason, meaning, purpose, ideal, and morality are the very negation of life.

Nietzsche is nihilistic and voluntaristic. By refusing to submit to reason, the will irrevocably becomes the instrument of the vilest instincts; it justifies every political ideology, from fascism to socialism.

Nietzsche is pleased that in his time the Dionysian element is finally reappearing after many centuries of oppression. He sees in Wagner a great artist in whose person the great Attic tragedy is being reborn. Nietzsche praises the opera *Tristan and Isolde* and has high hopes for the German composer. In *The Birth of Tragedy*, he praises Wagner, who admires Nietzsche's work in turn.

But in 1878, Nietzsche completed his book *Human, Too Human* just as Wagner was finishing the libretto for *Parsifal*. Without consulting each other first, they sent each other their new creations. Wagner's creation is about salvation: all his heroes save each other. What a horror to Nietzsche! In tragedy, no one saves anyone. The heroes suffer and say a resounding "Yes!" to their suffering. From this moment, Nietzsche broke with Wagner. He began to consider himself the sole representative of the Dionysian renaissance.

Schopenhauer wanted to free himself from life, consisting of only suffering and pain, by negating his own will to live, and longed for a kind of nirvana. Nietzsche joyfully accepted pain and suffering because to him it

---

10. Nietzsche, *Beyond Good and Evil*, preface.

is life itself. Schopenhauer was pessimistic; Nietzsche, tragically pessimistic. Schopenhauer escaped life by choosing asceticism, by turning to Eastern philosophy, by repressing the will. Nietzsche sought in pain itself the energy to laugh and to dance.

Schopenhauer's Eastern ethics were not in line with Nietzsche's metaphysics of the all-powerful Will. For Nietzsche, the will took precedence not only metaphysically ("In the beginning was the Will"), but also ethically ("One must live according to the Will, not against it").

As we have said before, the identification of pain with life was Nietzsche's way of hiding his vulnerability, his suffering, his despair.

The Death of God

The death of God is the central concept of Nietzsche's philosophy. "God is dead!" This is the German philosopher's most famous quote. It first appears in *The Gay Science* (1882). The author tells a parable in which a madman lights a lantern in broad daylight and wanders around the marketplace shouting: "I am looking for God! I'm looking for God!" The crowd laughs, but the madman stares at them and says: "Where has God gone? We killed him, you and I! We are all his murderers!"[11]

Nietzsche is not trying to prove that God is a figment of the human imagination. "God is dead" is a diagnosis. European civilization has murdered God. During

---

11. F. Nietzsche, *The Gay Science*, bk. 3, aphorism 125 ("The Madman").

his madness, around 1890, he wrote: "Mother, I did not kill Jesus, that was already done."[12]

For Nietzsche, "God is dead" is a joyful knowledge because it is information, a science that allows man to become god himself.

In Fyodor Dostoyevsky's novel *The Devils*, published in 1871, ten years before *The Gay Science*, Alexei Nilyich Kirilov had already proclaimed, "If God does not exist, then I am God." For Dostoyevsky the "death of God" is a dramatic fact; for Nietzsche it is a whole program of life.

Nietzsche observed the great men of his time closely and was struck by their calmness. Did they not understand that by rejecting God they must at the same time reject everything that flows from the idea of God?, he thought. He believed that everything that had been built on Christianity must be destroyed; that all European values, everything in any way connected with the idea of God, must be reconsidered.

The death of God means that a "re-reading" of man and the world (God's creation) becomes absolutely necessary.

The Superman

If the ideal model of man ceases to exist, if his eternal and unchanging nature disappears, then man is subject to evolution; he becomes "that which must shall be

---

12. Quoted in Robert Maggiori, "Mort parce que bête," *Libération*, July 23, 1998, https://www.liberation.fr/cahier-special/1998/07/23/un-ete-98-un-poche-par-jour-un-autre-caleconfriedrich-nietzsche-mort-parce-que-bete-introduction-et-_242170/.

overcome."[13] For Nietzsche, the death of God meant the death of man. And he rejoiced in it.

The superman is a Nietzschean concept that appears for the first time in his *Zarathustra* (1883). Nietzsche announces the birth of a new race that will emerge from man, but which will infinitely surpass him: the race of supermen. The superman must surpass man as much as man has surpassed the ape.

Man is a bridge, a transition. One can only love in man that which is transitory. The meaning of man *is* the superman.

The fundamental characteristic of the superman is the will to power. He dominates the "plebs" and rules the world. According to Nietzsche, the "great personality," the "noble personality," the "aristocrat" is a domineering being without morals, without virtue, and without compassion.

Nietzsche is not a nationalist; he wants to create an international race of lords who rule the earth. He does not venerate the state: he venerates the "hero." The misfortune of an entire nation, he says, is less important than the suffering of a great personality.

Although Nietzsche repeatedly mentions Dostoyevsky's novel *Crime and Punishment*, Raskolnikov and the superman are very different natures, almost at odds with each other. Raskolnikov is powerless. He is a penniless student, tormented by doubts and indecision. He

---

13. Nietzsche, *Thus Spoke Zarathustra*, bk. 1, Zarathustra's Prologue, 3.

craves power, but this craving comes from a deep sense of inferiority. Raskolnikov commits his crime to prove to himself that he is worth something. Nietzsche's superman is not the Raskolnikov of *Crime and Punishment* (1866) but rather the Pyotr Verkhovensky of *The Devils* (1872). Dostoyevsky was working on this novel at the same time Nietzsche was beginning to write his works. Dostoyevsky did not know Nietzsche, but he prefigured him.

Nietzsche tried to combine the notion of the superman with that of the "eternal return," which he had intuited in 1881, before he formulated the doctrine of the superman. The "eternal return" is a worldview according to which everything that happens in the world repeats itself indefinitely. Everyone must be prepared to live the same life an infinite number of times. With the appearance of the superman, the eternal return takes on a more precise meaning: only he who has created the preconditions for his return—the superman—returns. This, according to Nietzsche, is the meaning of existence: to be a superman who returns eternally.

The Last Man

Nietzsche rejoiced in the death of God but deplored the existence of the eternal bourgeois who continued to adhere to the values born of Christianity. According to Nietzsche, modern man, tired of living, prefers comfort and security; the "last man" is the goal that European civilization seems to have set for itself.

Nietzsche's last man is the antithesis of the superman. He is a pacifist and a conformist. Among the last men, there are no longer distinctions between rulers and subjects, the strong and the weak, the exceptional and the mediocre. There are no more social conflicts. All live the same life in a superficial and pitiful harmony. In their world, individuality, originality, and creativity are severely suppressed.

The last man continues to bear the burden of the old values. He realizes that his behavior is meaningless because God is dead. He then tries to forget himself in vain activism, in the search for profit and thrills.

In Nietzsche's world, we must free ourselves once and for all from traditional values, from the vestiges of Christian civilization. Become what you want! Be the creator of yourself! The consequences of the death of God must be manifested in all their amplitude.

Critique of Christianity

Nietzsche heralded that Christianity must be condemned for its denial of "noble bestiality, the instincts of war and conquest, the deification of passions, vengeance, anger, sensuality."[14] All these good things Christianity declares bad.

Christianity seeks to pacify the human heart, he posited. This pacification is dramatic: the wild beast, when tamed, loses all its grandeur.

---

14. B. Russell, *History of Western Philosophy* (1946), chap. 25.

According to Nietzsche, the history of the world is the eternal confrontation of "active" forces and "reactive" forces, those that only know how to react to external impulses. These two types of forces correspond to two types of morality: that of the "masters" and that of the "slaves." The master morality is an affirmation of life; the slave morality is the product of envy and hatred toward the masters, the fruit of a feeling of powerlessness, humiliation, and fear.

Slave morality is the morality of "resentment." Resentment is a hidden hatred that the weak harbor toward the strong. The history of Christianity is the history of the envious and resentful slave. The slave morality is self-defense: I pretend to love my neighbor because I fear that he will hurt me. If I were stronger and more courageous, I would openly show my contempt for him. To keep the strong on a leash, Nietzsche believed, Christians invented pity and compassion.

Vulnerable, desperate, hateful, Nietzsche could not believe in love. The "noble" man, whom he convinced himself he was, is, in reality, devoid of compassion. He is a ruthless, cunning, and wicked being concerned only with his own power.

LIVING ACCORDING TO NIETZSCHE

Nietzsche created the political voluntarist, the superman.

The superman wants to be above everyone, to dominate the "plebs" and rule the world. His goal is power. To achieve this goal, he is prepared to do anything.

continued

LIVING ACCORDING TO NIETZSCHE *continued*

The superman is nihilistic. He despises truth, goodness, beauty, love, and mercy. He despises reason, the heart, conscience, and virtue.

The superman believes only in his will. He does not believe in ideology (liberalism, communism, fascism, gender ideology), but he does not despise it because it can be useful to justify his power and his crimes.

The superman reads the works of Nietzsche; the last man reads Rousseau. The superman learns to manipulate the masses; the last man learns to be the mass. The superman spits on reason in the name of the Will; the last man spits on reason in the name of the Heart. The superman is a voluntarist; the last man is a sentimentalist. One is the proud lord and the other, the happy slave. . . .

The media preach the cult of the superman who "professionally" manages billions of mere mortals; at the same time, they promote the cult of the last man, the happy consumer incapable of creating anything. Modern culture is proud of both.

Part 2
THE BUILDERS

1

BLAISE PASCAL'S REASONS OF THE HEART
(1623–1662)

BLAISE PASCAL WAS BORN in Clermont-Ferrand, France, on June 19, 1623, to Étienne Pascal, president of the court of appeals responsible for tax disputes, and Antoinette Begon, daughter of a royal officer in the province of Auvergne. A family of the local nobility, the Pascals held important positions in the Auvergne judicial system for generations.

Étienne and Antoinette had three children: Gilberte, Blaise, and Jacqueline. Blaise was in poor health and suffered from various illnesses throughout his life.

Antoinette died when Blaise was three years old. Étienne found himself alone with three young children. His grief was immense. Preferring not to remarry, he devoted himself entirely to the education of his children. He was not particularly pious, but his faith was sincere. In 1631, the family moved to Paris.

Blaise was a gifted child. Étienne decided to homeschool the boy and served as his only teacher. He carefully worked out a learning curriculum: he would not teach him Latin and Greek until he was twelve, nor mathematics until he was fifteen. Having familiarized his son with linguistics, Étienne regularly conversed with him on the natural sciences. The boy enjoyed these conversations and was curious and perceptive. When he was twelve, he asked his father to teach him mathematics. Étienne, fearing that math would interfere with the study of Latin and Greek, promised to return to the subject later. One day, Étienne caught Blaise drawing some geometrical figures on the ground. He was amazed: his son was proving Euclid's thirty-second theorem on the sum of the angles of a triangle. Étienne abandoned his initial training plan and allowed Blaise to read books about math.

When Pascal wrote his *Treatise on Conic Sections*—at the age of sixteen—Descartes was informed of the miracle. Descartes, twenty-seven years older than Pascal, tried to hide his astonishment—and resentment.

In 1638, the government led by Cardinal Richelieu, whose coffers were ravaged by wars and embezzlement, decided to reduce the return on capital invested in the construction of Paris' city hall. Among the investors was Étienne Pascal, who put almost all of his fortune into the project. The investors were indignant and organized meetings in which the government was openly attacked. Richelieu, who did not tolerate the slightest rebellion, ordered Étienne and three other rentiers to be imprisoned in the Bastille. Étienne, warned in time by a friend, fled to Auvergne. His friends appealed to Louis XIII, but the king, timid and hesitant, did not dare interfere in the affairs of his chief minister.

The affair suddenly took a new turn. Cardinal Richelieu ordered that a group of children should perform

Georges de Scudéry's tragicomedy *Tyrannical Love* in his presence. The operation was entrusted to the Duchess of Aiguillon, who knew the Pascal family well and had long noticed the theatrical abilities of Jacqueline, who was only thirteen years old at the time.

In the absence of her father, Gilberte, who was just eighteen, took on the role of head of the family. When the Duchess asked her if she would allow her younger sister to take part in the play, she replied straight away, "Monsieur le Cardinal doesn't give us enough pleasure for us to take care of him!"[1] The Duchess was not convinced by this argument: "Understand that this occasion would surely result in your father's return!"

Gilberte said she would give the matter some thought and promised to respond after consulting Étienne's closest friends. They agreed Jacqueline should play the role. She did. The cardinal found her enchanting. She approached the cardinal and declaimed for him an epilogue in verse which she herself had composed:

> Do not be surprised, incomparable Armand, that I give so little pleasure to your eyes and ears. My soul is in great alarm. Bring my unfortunate father back from exile, save an innocent! Thus, you will give freedom to my mind and body, to my voice and movements, and you will make me capable of pleasing you!

The cardinal, deeply moved, raised the girl up, kissed her, and said, "Well, my child, tell your father that

---

1. *La vie de Monsieur Paschal, escrite par Madame Perier*, Bibliothèque Mazarine, 4546, translation from French.

he can come back with all confidence, and that I am very comfortable returning him to such a kind family."

The Duchess of Aiguillon then praised Étienne Pascal: "He is an honest and erudite man. It is a pity that his knowledge and his diligence are going to waste. And his son, Blaise, is only sixteen years old, and is already a great mathematician!"

Jacqueline, emboldened by her success, turned again to the cardinal. "I have one more favor to ask of Your Eminence."

"What is it, my child?"

"I beg Your Eminence to allow my father the honor of thanking you personally for your kindness."

"Not only do I allow him to do so, but I would like to receive him with his whole family."

Étienne promptly returned to Paris and presented himself to the cardinal, with his children.

"I have heard of your virtues and your merits," said Richelieu. "I am happy to give you back to a family that deserves your full attention."[2]

Two years later, Étienne was appointed to the important position of the king's agent in the province of Normandy. The family moves to Rouen. Blaise assists his father in the distribution of taxes and duties. Confronted with the traditional methods of calculation and finding them impractical, Pascal invented the first calculating machine, the Pascaline.

---

2. *La vie de Monsieur Paschal, escrite par Madame Perier*, Bibliothèque Mazarine, 98.

Pascal was one of the founders of mathematical analysis, probability theory, and projective geometry. He became the author of the fundamental law of hydrostatics. Pascal's scientific works were far superior to those of his contemporaries in their clarity and accessibility.

In 1646, through the doctors who treated Étienne for a dislocated hip, Pascal's family encountered Jansenism, a recent movement, based on the writings of the Dutch bishop Cornelius Jansenius. It was a reaction to the spread of materialist and bourgeois values among Catholics. It had some points in common with Calvinism: according to the Jansenists, mankind is entirely corrupted by original sin; on earth everything is sinful; and there is nothing honest and noble in the world, for it is ruled by the devil. No one can be saved except by grace. God gives his grace to the elect. The elect are those Christians whose lives are characterized by strict morals, hatred of the flesh and the body (even to the point of despising the sacrament of marriage), and the negation of joy, art, and beauty. The elect are few in number, and they are predestined.

Jansenism did not abolish the sacraments and did not deny the primacy of Peter. The Jansenists emphasized their Catholicity but interpreted St. Augustine's teaching on grace and predestination *radically*. Cornelius Jansenius had not suspected the uproar that his book *Augustinus* would provoke; his work would not have become the basis of a religious movement if the Jesuits, seeking to defend the doctrine of our free participation in our salvation, had not declared him a heretic.

Étienne's doctors introduced Blaise to another book by Jansenius—*Discourse on the Reformation of the Inner Man*. Pascal was a believer, but until then he had never shown any zeal for matters of faith. After reading the *Discourse,* he decided to live a truly Christian life, to pray, and to help the poor, orphans, and widows. This is what his biographers usually call his "first conversion."

Pascal did not see his conversion as a purely personal matter and tried to convert his family. Gilberte had recently married, but the beautiful and talented Jacqueline, whose poems provoked Cornelius' praise, was seriously thinking, under her brother's influence, of renouncing the world.

Pascal's health deteriorated considerably. Marguerite Perrier, Gilberte's daughter, recounts:

> The spirits having risen too strongly in my uncle's brain, he found himself in a sort of paralysis from the waist down, so that he was reduced to walking only with crutches; his legs and feet became cold as marble, and we were obliged to put slippers soaked in brandy on him every day to try to bring back the warmth to his feet.[3]

It seems that Pascal suffered from several illnesses at once—brain cancer, intestinal tuberculosis, and chronic rheumatism.

On one of his rare visits to France, Descartes met Pascal. He advised him to drink strong broth several

---

3. M. Perier, *Mémoire sur la vie de M. Pascal écrit par Mademoiselle Marguerite Perier, sa nièce* [Memoir of the life of Pascal written by Marguerite Perier, his niece*], translation from French, https://fr.wikisource.org/wiki/M%C3%A9moire_sur_la_vie_de_M._Pascal.

times a day and to stay in bed in the morning until he was tired of being sedentary (a custom Descartes had cherished throughout his life).

While Blaise was busy immersing himself in physics, Jacqueline was becoming increasingly pious. She dreamed of entering the convent of Port-Royal which, in the seventeenth century, was the main citadel of Jansenism in France. Her brother supported her, but Étienne, who was very attached to his daughter, asked her not to enter Port-Royal until after his death.

Étienne Pascal died on September 24, 1651. Blaise was twenty-eight years old, Jacqueline twenty-five. As she was preparing to leave for Port-Royal to commence her vocation, Blaise begged her not to leave him. She left anyway. In March, she wrote him a letter, begging him not to oppose her vocation: "I am addressing you, as the one upon whom my fate depends, to implore you: do not take from me that for which you cannot compensate. . . . If you do not have the strength to follow me, at least refrain from holding me back; do not destroy what you have built."[4]

Blaise was forced to come to terms with the situation. He was overwhelmed by grief and anxiety. He prayed and went to church less often; meanwhile, his reputation as a scholar only grew. The doors of the most famous aristocratic salons opened to him. The awareness of his genius awakened his pride. At the home of the Duke of Roannez, his close friend and future business partner, Blaise came

---

4. Michel Le Guern, "Les lettres de Jacqueline Pascal," *Revue d'Histoire litteraire de la France* 103, no. 2 (2003): pp. 267–273.

into contact with the cream of society. Queen Christina of Sweden, having quickly forgotten "her" Descartes, who had died two years earlier, became interested in Pascal's works and corresponded with him. He sent her the calculating machine he invented—the Pascaline—as a gift.

On June 5, 1653, when Jacqueline took the monastic veil, Pascal was suffering from an inner emptiness. He conceived a growing aversion to secular society. He was also consumed by remorse: he had not obeyed the call that had resounded in his soul eight years before; he had not been able to overcome his thirst for knowledge, nor his vanity. He knew he needed a real conversion, but this conviction was purely intellectual; his heart was not in it.

During the night of November 23, 1654, Pascal, at the age of thirty-one, had a mystical experience, which he would call his "night of fire":

> Fire.
>
> God of Abraham, God of Isaac, God of Jacob, not
> of the philosophers and the scholars.
>
> Certitude. Certitude. Feeling. . . .
>
> God of Jesus Christ. . . .
>
> Greatness of the human soul. . . .
>
> Joy, joy, joy, tears of joy. . . .
>
> Jesus Christ. . . .
>
> I fled from him, abandoned him, crucified
> him. . . . I left him.
>
> Let me never be separated from him.
>
> This is eternal life, that they know you, the one true
> God, and the one that you sent, Jesus Christ. . . .

> It is kept only through the ways taught in the
> Gospel:
> Renunciation, total and sweet. . . .
> Amen.

After he recovered, he scribbled these words in a rough draft, then copied them onto a piece of parchment which he sewed into the lining of his garment. He never parted with this relic, which his biographers call the *Memorial*.[5] The parchment was discovered in Gilberte's house after her brother's death.

With passionate conviction, Pascal rebelled against himself and his old ambition to scientifically discover the meaning of life and the salvation of the soul.

Although Pascal left many texts with religious content to posterity, none of them penetrates the philosopher's personality as well as his *Memorial*. The "Night of Fire" was a decisive turning point in his life. He did not even tell Jacqueline what happened. He broke with society and left Paris for Port-Royal.

The French bishops, strongly influenced by the Society of Jesus, condemned Jansenism. The entourage of Louis XIV wanted to close Port-Royal. At the request of Antoine Arnauld, the spiritual leader of the monastery, Pascal undertook to defend Port-Royal with his pen. With his unerring strategic eye, he understood that the Jansenists could not win the battle on the terrain of dogmatic subtleties, which the public would not understand.

---

5. https://www.ccel.org/ccel/pascal/memorial.i.html

So fought on different terrain—that of moral principles. He attacked the casuistry of the Jesuits and the "flexibility" of their morality. He published *Provincial Letters*, the first of which dates from January 23, 1656. They were widely printed and distributed throughout France, found, even in the office of Cardinal Mazarin, who in 1642 succeeded Richelieu as chief minister to the king. It was a highly successful gambit. Pascal convinced public opinion of the justice of Port-Royal's cause. Repression followed: some of the publishers were imprisoned and Pascal was forced to temporarily go into hiding. But the monastery remained open.

For several years, Pascal conceived the idea of composing an *Apologia for Christianity*. In 1657, he began to take notes and classify them according to subject. He gave himself ten years to write the book.

Illness made his task difficult, and his doctors forbade him any mental activity. Nevertheless, he continued to write, and on a range of subjects. After his death, his Jansenist friends discovered his notes. Roughly a thousand of them, of varying genres, scope, and degree of completion, survived. They were deciphered and published first under the title *Thoughts on Religion and Other Subjects*, and later under the simpler name of *Pensées* ("thoughts"). The work is mainly about God's relationship with mankind. What is striking about the *Pensées* is their depth and originality. Pascal is the only great mathematician of modern times who is also a great writer.

In reading the *Pensées*, one understands that Pascal is Jansenist in his perception of the original Fall and its dramatic consequences: he emphasizes the *corruption* of human nature, whereas traditional Catholic teaching speaks of the original *wound* caused by sin. In the *Pensées*, however, Pascal does not dwell on our wretchedness but, rather, emphasizes our possibilities. He is as much concerned with *the greatness of man with God* as with *the misery of man without God*.

Pascal accepts in its entirety the teaching of the great Father of the Church, St. Augustine, whereas the Jansenists accepted only certain of Augustine's statements about grace and predestination. Pascal restored in the Catholic consciousness St. Augustine's view of the heart, written in his *Confessions*: God is not just reason and will; he is also heart. Concupiscence and egoism may, as Calvinists and Jansenists believe, stem from the heart, but so do freedom, morality, and spirituality. Pascal's mysticism and philosophy of life were alien to the spirit of Port-Royal.

Pascal admired the piety, courage, and "radicalism" of the Jansenists he had met in Rouen and at Port-Royal. He admired their will, their heroic struggle against civil authority, their thirst for independence and freedom, but he strongly differed from them in his love of the world.

In 1658, his health deteriorated. In 1660—at thirty-seven—he looked like an old man, unable to write, read, or think cogently. He accepted suffering as a gift from God.

Louis XIV, deeply annoyed by the refusal of the Jansenists to accept any compromise in matters of religion, told Mazarin that he had decided to get rid of the Jansenists.

At the king's insistence, in the spring of 1661, the Council of State approved the decision of the Assembly of the French Clergy requiring every priest and monk to sign a statement condemning five theological propositions attributed to Jansenius.

The Jansenists had difficulty reaching an agreement. The group, led by Arnauld, tried to draw up reservations to the statement that would allow them to sign with a clear conscience: in Arnauld's opinion, the propositions in question did not appear in Jansenius' book. Another group, to which Blaise and Jacqueline belonged, refused to sign. The majority supported Arnauld's opinion. Jacqueline resisted as long as she could, but finally signed. Her remorse tortured her, exhausted her, and finally killed her. She died two months later at the age of thirty-six. Blaise, prostrate with grief, collapsed.

In the autumn of 1661, the Assembly of the Clergy removed all possibility of amending the statement. Arnauld and the monks allied with him, still seeking a way out, condemned Blaise's intransigence. This was too much for Blaise, who then broke with Port-Royal.

Pascal fell ill and called for the parish priest, who came and heard his confession. The priest came often, and Blaise confessed each time he came. Recalling their meetings, the priest later wrote: "I admired Monsieur Pascal's patience, modesty, charity, and great abnegation. . . . He was as obedient as a child."[6]

---

6. *La vie de Monsieur Paschal, escrite par Madame Perier*, Bibliothèque Mazarine, 115.

Pascal knew he was on the verge of death. He begged for the sacrament of the Eucharist to be brought to him. The doctors assured him that his condition was not critical. On August 17, at midnight, he had violent convulsions. When they ceased, everyone thought he was dead. Gilberte suffered because her brother could not receive the Holy Communion he was longing for. But Blaise regained consciousness just as the priest appeared on the doorstep. He approached the dying man, handed him Communion, and said, "Here is the one you wanted so much." Pascal received Communion and spoke his last words: "May God never leave me!"[7] The convulsions started again, and he lost consciousness. On August 19, 1662, Blaise Pascal surrendered his soul to God.

His life was so intense that Jean Racine, the illustrious playwright, remarked, not without humor, "Monsieur Pascal died of old age at thirty-nine!"[8]

"There was a genius," wrote François-René de Chateaubriand,

> who, at the age of twelve, with bars and rings, created mathematics; who, at sixteen, composed the ablest treatise on conic sections that had appeared since the time of the ancients; who, at nineteen, created a machine [the Pascaline] that could do what

---

[7]. *La vie de Monsieur Paschal, escrite par Madame Perier*, Bibliothèque Mazarine, 116.

[8]. Armand Jardillier, *Les "carrosses a cinq solz" de Monsieur Blaise Pascal* (Paris, 1962), https://excerpts.numilog.com/books/9782307295662.pdf, translation from French.

previously only the mind could do; who, at twenty-three, demonstrated the phenomenon of the air's gravity, thereby overthrowing one of the great errors of ancient physics; who, at the age when intellectual faculties have hardly begun to expand in others, having gone through the whole cycle of human sciences, discovered their inanity and turned all his thoughts toward religion; who, from that moment until his death (in his thirty-ninth year), amid incessant bodily infirmities, set the language Bossuet and Racine spoke. . . . Finally, who, in his brief intervals of ease, resolved, unassisted, one of the profoundest problems of geometry, and randomly committed to paper thoughts no less worthy of God than of man. The name of this stupendous genius was Blaise Pascal.[9]

Pascal was "a philosopher outside of philosophy." He considered himself a man of science and did not claim to be a philosopher, but few men of science made a greater contribution to philosophy.

The Personality of Pascal

Rousseau praised pure, innocent human nature even while living in filth; Pascal, by contrast, felt in his heart the dramatic consequence of mankind's original Fall, but he led a noble, demanding, and holy life.

The striking thing about Pascal's personality was the balance he struck between heart, reason, and the will.

---

9. F.-R. de Chateaubriand, *The Genius of Christianity* (1802), chap. 6.

Pascal was a person of heart, but his heart did not absorb his reason or stifle his will. He was not a sentimentalist; he possessed in abundance the virtues of the intellect and the will. He was a poet who was also a scholar and an ascetic. His heart was not, like Rousseau's, a rag blown by the wind: it was wise, bold, enduring, temperate, and just.

Through his life, Pascal teaches us to cultivate noble feelings, renouncing sentimentality as much as rationalist and voluntarist insensitivity.

The strength of Pascal's philosophy is his spirit and personality. Pascal is both fire and grace. His philosophy is not a doctrine, but a life. It tends to inflame a person's heart and will, even more than it illuminates his mind.

Voltaire understood Pascal so well, he feared him. He wrote, "I have long wanted to fight this giant."[10] He did so, but in vain: Pascal's moral superiority is too obvious. His heart and will are stronger, and his intelligence purer and more convincing. Voltaire, in bad faith, distorts the meaning of Pascal's *Pensées* by detaching them from their context, eliminating anything that might contradict his argument, and retaining only the most pessimistic aspects. He feigns ignorance of Pascal's belief that the misery of man *without* God paves the way for the greatness of man *with* God.

The Reasons of the Heart

For Pascal, the heart is the foundation of reason and the will. The heart does not only *feel*, but it also *knows* and *wants*.

---

10. Voltaire, Letter to Formont (1733).

This understanding of the heart stems from the Bible, in which the heart is the center of the body-soul-spirit triad. The heart is a physical, psychic, and spiritual force.

Neither Plato nor Aristotle had considered the heart as a spiritual faculty distinct from the intellect and the will. For Aristotle, the heart was limited to the physiological and psychic spheres, to the irrational world that man shares with animals. The ancient Greeks inspired the notion that the spiritual attributes of the heart are transferred to the intellect and the will.

According to St. Augustine in his *Confessions*, the heart was both a physical and a spiritual faculty, even if it took a back seat to reason and the will. But from the twelfth century onward, it was Aristotle and his minimalist vision of the heart that set the tone in Europe. It is not until Pascal, in the seventeenth century, that the "question of the heart" returns to the agenda.

The heart is the foundation of reason. It grasps immediately and intuitively the existence of things which cannot be logically proved. Thus, the heart establishes the point of departure for reasoning and knowing. It enables us to grasp first principles, such as space, time, movement, number. Our knowledge of them is even more solid than that which we get from reasoning. As Pascal says in his *Pensées*,

> Principles are intuited, propositions are inferred, all of them with certainty, although in different ways. And it is as useless and absurd for reason to demand of the heart proof of its first principles, before consenting to them, as it would be for the heart to

demand of reason an intuitive grasp of all demonstrated propositions before accepting them.[11]

For Pascal, the certainties of the heart are often firmer than the mathematical certainties so beloved of Descartes.

The heart is the foundation not only of reason but also of the will: it gives our life, immediately and intuitively, a *purpose*, which, in turn, gives direction to the will (the fundamental choice, often unconscious, between the Creator and creatures, between God and the self).

For Pascal, Holy Scripture is the "science of the heart." As such, Judeo-Christianity is a religion of the heart. At the center of our relationship with God is the heart. God acts first in our heart, then in our intellect and in our will. The heart is the locus of communion between God and man. It merges with our mind and will so that we might know God, man, and the world in love and in truth.

Man Is a Thinking Reed

Pascal studied man as passionately and diligently as he studied geometry. François Mauriac says Pascal is "the only humanist worthy of this beautiful name; the only one who denies man nothing; he goes through the whole of man to attain God."[12]

---

11. Pascal, *Pensées* (1670), section 4, "On the Means of Belief," no. 284.
12. F. Mauriac, *Blaise Pascal et sa sœur Jacqueline* [Blaise Pascal and his sister Jacqueline*] (Paris: Hachette, 1931).

For Pascal, one cannot speak of the greatness of man without also speaking of his nothingness; and one cannot speak of man's nothingness without also speaking of his greatness. Pascal's humanism is broad, extreme, and dramatic, whereas the humanism of the Enlightenment is narrow and naive.

For Pascal, it is not reason but God who reveals man to man. Without God, we can appreciate neither our greatness nor our nothingness.

> What then will you become, O men! who try to find out by your natural reason what is your true condition? . . . Know then, proud man, what a paradox you are to yourself. Humble yourself, weak reason; be silent, foolish nature; learn that man infinitely transcends man, and learn from your Master your true condition, of which you are ignorant.[13]

Pascal surmised that man is a spiritual being and a son of God (hence his greatness), but he is also a sinful creature (hence his weakness). Adam and Eve committed sin. This corrupted human nature. The person who is unaware of his sinful nature (or chooses to ignore it), lives in darkness: "It is astonishing that the mystery farthest removed from our knowledge concerns the transmission of sin, without which we can know nothing about ourselves."[14]

According to Pascal, there are only two periods in history: before the Fall and after the Fall. Since the Fall,

---

13. Pascal, *Pensées,* no. 434.
14. Pascal, *Pensées*, no. 434.

human nature has not changed. Man, he writes, is full of faults, and this is an obvious evil; but it is an even greater evil for him to ignore his faults and live willfully in the illusion of perfection. Pascal attacks the as yet unborn ideology of *progress*, of which Rousseau, with his denial of original sin, would become one of the initiators. Pascal can be understood as a response not only to Descartes' rationalism but to the naive optimism of the Enlightenment that would emerge soon after Pascal's death. Europe would live for almost two centuries on the illusion of the absolute goodness of humanity and on the illusion of moral progress stemming from scientific knowledge.

Pascal comments on Epictetus, the stoic, and Montaigne, the skeptic. The former, aware of man's greatness but unaware of his weakness, is *presumptuous* in that he believes he can accomplish God's will by his own strength; the latter, aware of man's weakness but unaware of his greatness, is *pusillanimous*. He proposes a life of pleasure, convenience, and repose. To know God without knowing anything of our own nothingness leads to *pride*; to know of our own nothingness but to know nothing of God leads to *despair*.

In *Pensées*, Pascal situates man between "Zero and Infinity":

> Man is a reed, the weakest thing in nature, but he is a thinking reed. It does not take the entire universe to arm itself to crush it; steam, a drop of water is enough to kill it. But if the universe were to crush him, man would be even nobler than what kills him because he knows that he is dying and that the advantage the

universe has over him, the universe knows nothing about. All our dignity consists then in thought. It is from there that we must rise and not from space and duration which we cannot fill. Let us endeavor then to think well: that is the principle of morality.[15]

It is not in space that we must seek our dignity, and not in the possession of material goods, but rather in right thinking: "Through space, the universe encompasses and swallows me up like an atom; through thought, I comprehend the world."[16]

Thought is a notion that would seem to bring Pascal closer to Descartes; however, this is not so. In Pascal's view, man is not only "thought," as Descartes conceived it: he is "thought" guided by the heart and by the will. The dignity of man is not in "pure" thought but in the moral orientation of that thought.

Man, says Pascal, instead of thinking well, seeks to forget himself in entertainment, to divert his thoughts from the existential questions. He kills time, until time, in turn, kills him.

"Pascal has never been more necessary to us than today," says Albert Béguin. "He was perhaps the first to know what Berdyaev said Dostoyevsky knew so well: that the question of God is *a question of man*."[17] Two

---

15. Pascal, *Pensées*, no. 347.

16. Pascal, *Pensées*, no. 348.

17. A. Béguin, ed., *Pascal par lui-même: images et textes présentés* [Pascal by himself: images and texts presented*] (Paris: Éditions de Seuil, 1958).

centuries before Dostoyevsky, Pascal spoke to us about God *in order to save man.*

God of Abraham . . .

Pascal's religious creed is that of his *Memorial*: "God of Abraham, God of Isaac, God of Jacob, not of the philosophers and the scholars." Pascal thirsts for the living God, the God of love.

For Pascal, God is not a concept, a self-contained abstraction, a self-contemplating thought. God is a relationship. God is love. Only Christ can lead to love. He alone can give meaning to our lives.

For him, the proof of God's existence is in the human heart. God is known through inner experience. Metaphysical proofs of God's existence are not convincing.

"Pascal, the believer," writes Jean Steinmann,

> is infinitely closer to today's unbelievers than is Voltaire, the skeptic. . . . The present world is riddled with anxiety. Man feels caught up in a monstrous drama. He is lost. He is alone in the face of death. Perhaps if Christianity had survived with all its medieval framework, Pascal would be less understood today, for he professes the Christian faith in its nakedness. He has detached it from all the social or metaphysical ties to which it seemed definitively linked under the *Ancien Régime*. There is no metaphysics in Pascal as in Saint Thomas or Descartes; no childish cosmology, no throne [no king] supporting the altar [the

> Church] as in Bossuet. In a century of royal absolutism that linked faith to the social order, as it had once been to the Roman Empire, to Aristotle's physics, Pascal's judgements on politics and metaphysics were cruelly lucid. Faced with the Christ represented by a Church whose weaknesses he does not hide, his sharp sentences portray a man stripped of all masks, shivering because of the cold of an empty universe and to whom the choice is only between two extremes: the Crucified One or nothingness.[18]

Pascal believed that, life without God is nothingness. Material goods and pleasure are worth nothing. By betting on the existence of God and eternal happiness ("Pascal's wager"), the doubting man has nothing to lose: if God does not exist, he loses only his nothingness.

Nietzsche would fall in ecstasy before Pascal's nothingness, but instead of Christ he offers us the Antichrist. Nietzsche abolishes man to make room for the superman; Pascal strips man to bring him closer to the living God.

Pascal continues to influence people's hearts. "I doubt that without him," François Mauriac admitted, "I would have remained faithful, or rather I have a hard time imagining what would have supported my fidelity in times of crisis, those of my own life, those of the lives of men."[19] Pascal's thoughts substantially changed

---

18. J. Steinmann, *Pascal* (Paris: Desclée de Brouwer, 1965), p. 150.

19. F. Mauriac, *What I Believe* (1952), chap. 8 ("The Debt to Pascal").

the worldview of Takashi Nagai (1908–1951), a Japanese radiologist who survived the atomic bombing of 1945 and became world famous after the publication of his book *The Bells of Nagasaki*. Under the influence of Pascal, Nagai converted to Christianity on the threshold of World War II. In 2017, Pope Francis declared that he wanted Pascal to be canonized. What interests the Jesuit pope is Pascal's personality and his love of Christ, not, of course, the old controversy between Jesuits and Jansenists.

Pascal is a mystic, but "however great he may be," writes Mauriac,

> he remains one of us. . . . He spoke our language to the end . . . God speaks to each of us through Pascal. It is precisely for us, and in a language suitable for us, that He uttered words which one night I hesitated to say before a huge crowd because they arose from the most intimate and most secret part of my being: "I thought of you in my suffering. Be consoled. You would not be looking for me if you had not found me. For you, I have shed a drop of blood. . . . I love you more fervently than you have loved your sins." It is in the confidence of a friend speaking to his friend that we should study what these words, from generation to generation, have given to those to whom they were addressed.[20]

---

20. Mauriac, *What I Believe*, chap. 8 ("The Debt to Pascal").

LIVING ACCORDING TO PASCAL

To live according to Pascal is to find one's heart, to accept it as the center of one's personality and as the foundation of one's intellect and will.

To live according to Pascal is to search constantly for truth and to communicate this truth to people with empathy and elegance.

To live according to Pascal is to be aware of one's misery without God and one's greatness with God. It is to live in the truth about oneself.

To live according to Pascal is to refuse to drown the emptiness of one's Godless existence in amusement, entertainment, professional activism, and other trivial pursuits.

To live according to Pascal is to be concerned about the salvation of one's soul. It is to be horrified by the spectacle of spiritual indifference.

To live according to Pascal is to live one's life heroically (by making radical choices) and not naively (lulled by the myth of Progress).

To live according to Pascal is to choose between Christ Crucified and nothingness.

2

THE AUTHENTIC LIFE OF SÖREN KIERKEGAARD
(1813–1855)

SÖREN KIERKEGAARD WAS BORN on May 5, 1813, in Copenhagen, Denmark. Michael, his father, was a wealthy merchant. He was fifty-six years old at the time of Sören's birth. His wife, Anne, was forty-four. Sören was the youngest child.

Anne once worked as Michael's servant. He married her after the death of his first wife.

Michael was a pious man with a melancholic temperament. He was dark and stern. A stifling atmosphere prevailed in the family. "From childhood I was subjected to an unbearable despotic power," Kierkegaard writes in his diary, "to a strict and austere Christian education which was, humanly speaking, madness."[1] Sören nevertheless loved his father dearly: "If you want to know how I became the writer I am, I will tell you that I owe it to that old man. It is to him above all that I owe what I am."[2]

---

1. S. Kierkegaard, *Journals*, 6:33, 75.
2. Kierkegaard, *Journals*, 7:381.

Sören lost his mother when he was six years old. His three older sisters and two brothers died in turn, either from illness or accident, none of them reaching the age of thirty-three. Only Sören and his older brother Peter survived.

In 1830, in accordance with his father's wishes, Sören entered the faculty of theology at the University of Copenhagen, where he studied Lutheran theology and German philosophy. He showed little interest in his studies. He led a frivolous life.

The sins of his father's youth remained a mystery to Sören for a long time. He learned of them when one evening his father, drunk, opened his heart to him. He was shocked, indeed traumatized. It was, he said, an "earthquake." Once, at the age of ten, his father, working then as a shepherd, cursed God when he was alone on the moor for making him to do particularly hard work. Sören also learned that his father had corrupted his servant, his future wife, by seducing her and getting her pregnant shortly after the death of his first wife. Kierkegaard concluded his siblings had died prematurely because his father's sins had brought down a curse on the family.

Michael died a few months after these revelations. He left Sören a large sum of money which enabled him to live comfortably and, in a few years, to finance the publication of his works.

In 1837, he met the fifteen-year-old Regine Olsen. In 1840, they became engaged. The day after his engagement, Kierkegaard already regretted what he had done. A year later to the day, he sent his engagement ring back to

Regine with a farewell letter: "Forgive him who is unable to make the girl happy."[3] Regine sank into despair.

Why did he break off the engagement? "Natural, spontaneous, charming," writes Sören, "she was in every way different from me, a melancholic; I had no other joy than to praise her beauty. . . . She chose life; I chose pain."[4]

Kierkegaard broke with Regine because making spiritual progress had become, for him, a matter of the greatest urgency. He chose a higher, more demanding, more exceptional destiny. He loved Regine ("what I have lost is the only thing I loved"), but he was convinced that a greater pact, "a pact of tears," bound him to God.[5]

Sören found this separation hard to bear. In a letter to Regine, which he did not send, he writes, "Thank you for everything I owe you; thank you for that time you were mine. . . . Thank you for your childlike simplicity . . . , thank you for all that you have taught me by your charm, if not by your wisdom."[6]

Later he would say, "I owe everything to the wisdom of an old man [Michael] and the simplicity of a young girl [Regine]."[7]

Six years after their breakup, Regine married Frederick Schlegel, her former teacher and admirer. "She got married,"

---

3. Kierkegaard, *Journals*, 6:15, 350.

4. Jean Grenier, "Sören Kierkegaard: Biographie," La République des Lettres, https://xn--rpubliquedeslettres-bzb.fr/kierkegaard.php.

5. Grenier.

6. Kierkegaard, *Journals*, 6:35, 244.

7. Kierkegaard, *Journals*, 6:35, 225.

Kierkegaard wrote later. "When I read the news in the paper, I had a kind of attack."[8] He wrote to Schlegel, "In this life she will belong to you, but she will go down in history with me."[9] Sören bequeathed his entire estate to Regine.

Two weeks after the breakup, Sören went to Berlin to attend Schelling's lectures. When he returned four months later, he began a new phase in his life—that of a writer.

Sören was becoming increasingly convinced of the truth of Christianity. At just this time, he renounced his ambition to become a pastor. The situation recalled his renunciation of marriage after having fallen in love with Regine. He sought to limit his life in order to intensify it. Sören made *existential* choices.

He distanced himself from worldly life. He moved into a spacious house, with a secretary and a valet. "I live in my room like a besieged person, not wanting to see anyone and constantly fearing the invasion of the enemy: visitors."[10] Every day he would walk the rainy streets of Copenhagen in his top hat, smoking a cigar and often making ironic remarks to passersby.

Kierkegaard's capacity for work was astonishing. He wrote seven books in five years. He was an exceptionally gifted person. The power of images and metaphors, his poetic imagination, precise psychological analysis, irony, preacher's pathos, and acerbic denunciation—these Kierkegaard brought to bear in order to convince his readers.

---

8. Kierkegaard, *Journals*, 6:5–6, 88.

9. Kierkegaard, *Journals*, 6:35, 231.

10. Grenier.

All his works, whether aesthetic, philosophical, or religious, are the volcanic eruptions of a seething introspection. He is the precursor of the philosophical trend that would later be called "existentialism."

In 1843, at the age of thirty, he published a major work—*Either/Or* (also known as *The Alternative*)—in which he set forth, for the first time, his vision of the different stages of existence. Over the next two years, he published *Fear and Trembling* (1843), *Repetition* (1843), *Philosophical Fragments* (1844), *The Concept of Anxiety* (1844), and *Stages on Life's Way* (1845).

In 1845, the liberal, satirical newspaper *The Corsair*, which had a wide circulation, made Kierkegaard the subject of caricatures. On the streets of Copenhagen Sören was harassed by the taunts of passersby. Youths chased him, shouting "Either, or!" and threw stones at him. "If Copenhagen ever had a unanimous opinion about anyone, I must say it was about me: I am an idler and a loafer."

From 1851 onward, he wrote only his *Diary*.

In 1855, however, he took up his pen to denounce the hypocrisy of the Lutheran Church. He railed against the emasculation of Christian life and the pursuit of comfort, which he said was incompatible with the teachings of Christ.

This outburst was prompted by the death of the head of the Danish Lutheran Church, Bishop Mynster, who had been his father's spiritual director and thus very close to the Kierkegaard family. The Danish people loved this pastor and mourned his passing. Kierkegaard, on the other hand, said that he was not a Christian:

> A life of pleasure, free from suffering, humiliation, fears, and despair . . . does not give the right to bear witness to the truth. . . . The bearer of truth is the one who is poor, humiliated, and who does not complain, covered with curses and slanders, the one who is treated as an outcast.[11]

To be a Christian, Kierkegaard insisted, is to have a restless and rebellious spirit, to strive to save love crucified by an impious age. All want a quiet, settled, and happy life. The idea of Christianity is perverted; there is no more Christianity. Of all the heresies and schisms, there is no heresy more dangerous and subtle than "playing at Christianity."

The official press ridiculed Kierkegaard. His nerves were shot. On November 11, 1855, he fainted in the street. He died a few days later at the age of forty-two. The crowd saw in his death the hand of God.

Kierkegaard was little known and little appreciated during his lifetime. He became popular only in the twentieth century with the emergence of totalitarian regimes and the problems posed by the triumph of mass culture.

The Personality of Kierkegaard

Kierkegaard himself is the object of his philosophy. His life—his biography—is the subject of his reflection. Kierkegaard was interested in himself, and this interest was deeply moral. It was not egocentrism or

---

11. S. Kierkegaard, *Was Bishop Mynster a "Witness to the Truth"?* (1855).

navel-gazing, but an introspection whose aim was to form a theory of the self, an existential approach that could be useful not only for himself but also for others.

This introspection—this self-knowledge—helps us to emerge from anonymity in our relations with God and with people. In Kierkegaard there is no "we": there is only "you" and "me." In his philosophy the "way to yourself" becomes the way to God and to others.

Kierkegaard believed every encounter with the world provokes *fear* in the face of the magnitude of our own responsibility. We must choose, act, grow. We must be responsible for ourselves before God. *Despair* is the positive fruit of personal dissatisfaction, the fear of standing still. For Kierkegaard, fear and despair were not psychological but moral categories. Without fear and despair there would be no personal growth.

To be free, to choose, to fear and to despair, is what it means to exist for Kierkegaard. These few words define the essence of his personality.

The Primacy of the Singular

The main theme of Kierkegaard's life is the *existence* of the singular, individual, concrete person. The Danish philosopher was not interested in humanity "in general" but in the singular, *existential* experience of each individual.

Kierkegaard affirmed the primacy of the singular. Each individual life is a unique experience. One's existence is unrepeatable, inimitable. Every ephemeral thought, every fleeting feeling, every passing sensation is important. Theories and systems (the intellectual "whole"), like empires and kingdoms (the material "whole"), are worthless in the face of singular existence. This is what must concern the philosopher. It is in the singular that truth, life, and God himself are hidden.

The individual is infinitely superior to the collective. Kierkegaard's philosophy is a reaction to the Hegelian system in which the individual was only a means at the disposal of the Absolute Spirit to achieve its ends in history. In Hegelianism, the individual is sacrificed to this spirit. He must merge into the "anonymous whole," be it the state or abstract thought. In Hegel's view there is no individual freedom and responsibility, no authentic existence.

After the collapse of Nazism and Communism, which hated the singularity of human life and tried to dissolve it in the mass—in the party or the state—Kierkegaard's approach was an indispensable component of philosophical reflection following Auschwitz and Kolyma (the Gulag). In today's modern world plagued by new forms of totalitarianism (the ones offered by Rousseau are less obvious but just as cruel), reading Kierkegaard is a privileged means of spiritual uplift.

A Theory of the Self

Kierkegaard would say that I exist insofar as I am passionate about my singular existence. "In all that I have written," says Kierkegaard, "it is solely and exclusively about myself. . . . Man is me in relation to myself. I am my relation to myself."[12]

His belief was that interest in our individuality is not egocentrism. It is a necessary step toward self-knowledge and therefore toward humility, which is the virtue of those who live in truth about themselves.

Additionally, in order to grow, we must take an interest in ourselves and love ourselves. Self-love makes us better; it makes us deeply moral beings. It is through self-love that we arrive at love of God and love of others.

The Truth Is a Living and Personal Reality

For Kierkegaard, philosophical thought must not *be a thought in which the thinker does not exist*. Philosophy must not be a science. Science is only interested in concepts; it has no use for the "I" and the "you." Science proceeds by abstraction: it eliminates the concrete, the temporal, and personal experience to immerse itself in the conceptually ideal. It eliminates life! Science loves systems. Existence, the mode of being of the individual subject, is precisely the opposite of a system. To exist is to be present, incomplete, detached, outside of any system.

To *objective* truth, which is indifferent to whether it is recognized, Kierkegaard opposed *subjective* truth, which is a personal commitment. Objective truth only becomes subjective truth insofar as it forces us to change our lives. Subjective truth is a sign of sincerity and

---
12. Kierkegaard, *Journals*, 6:16, 2, 331.

authenticity. Becoming subjective is the highest mission assigned to us.

Contrary to what many authors have written, Kierkegaard is not a subjectivist philosopher: he does not make man the measure of all things. When he says that subjectivity is truth and truth is subjectivity, he means that truth is the correspondence between my objective knowledge and the way I embody it in my life. Truth is the authenticity of my life, not a true discourse on existence. Man "forgets to exist" when what he knows overwhelms and absorbs his heart: he who speaks of death as a concept and not as a reality capable of shattering his life for which he must prepare in some way, "forgets to exist."

The purpose of thought is not abstract reflection but something to be lived in real life. True knowledge is more than just information. What good does it do to know the world and everything in it if it does not somehow change my life? What counts is knowledge, inasmuch as it can transform my life.

The Philosopher Is Above All a Subject

Kierkegaard's philosophy was an attempt to make sense of his most intimate, personal experiences. It is difficult to find a philosopher whose life and work are so intimately linked. Hegel's *Science of Logic* or Kant's *Critique of Pure Reason* are very far from being expressions of their authors' lives. Kierkegaard's ideas, on the other hand, are so autobiographical that they faithfully reflect his life experience, his concerns, his feelings.

Why has philosophy in our time gone so far astray that it tells us nothing about the lives of its authors? Could it be because they themselves do not understand who they are? How can we understand the world if we cannot understand ourselves?

To Exist Is to Choose

To Kierkegaard, to exist is to realize oneself by freely choosing between several alternatives: "either/or." It is not, of course, a choice between a filet mignon or a steak, between an iPhone or an Android. It is an existential choice: life or death, freedom or slavery, faith or unbelief, loyalty or betrayal, love or selfishness.

In choosing, he surmised, we become aware of our personal dignity. If we fail to choose, if we let time and events effectively choose for us, we run the risk of losing our own selfhood.

Freedom breeds anxiety. "Anguish is the vertigo of freedom,"[13] says Kirkegaard. We must run the risk of choosing, of acting, of being wrong. Many people, in order to avoid "anguish," flee from freedom. They become alienated in all sorts of entertainments that make them forget the obligation to "exist."

The Stages of Existence

According to Kierkegaard, existence consists of three stages: the aesthetic, the ethical, and the religious.

---

13. S. Kierkegaard, *The Concept of Anxiety* (1844), part 2, no. 2.

Kierkegaard describes the course of his life and deduces from it the threefold structure of the life of every individual. According to these stages, he divides people into four types: the philistine, the aesthete, the ethicist, and the religious.

The *philistine* does not choose. He does not exist. He has no "self." He is a conformist. He swims with the current, accommodating himself to circumstances without thinking that he can change anything.

The *aesthete* chooses his own path: pleasure. He is a professional of desire. He lives in the moment. The moment does not belong to time: it is not the present; rather, it is the void. There is no unity in his life, no coherence to his existence. Kierkegaard was an aesthete during his university years.

The *ethicist* also chooses his own path: duty. Good and evil are the determining categories of his existence and behavior. He takes control of his own life. Unfortunately, the fulfillment of duty, in itself, does not make us happy; it is not the meaning of existence. The ethicist is a "tragic hero." Kierkegaard could be considered an ethicist during the several months he was engaged to Regine.

The *religious* man chooses to do the will of God. To accomplish it, he is capable of doing the opposite of what duty demands of him. God asked Abraham to kill his son Isaac as a sacrifice to him, and Abraham did so. This was a violation of ethics, a violation of the commandment "thou shalt not kill." God substituted himself for ethics. Faith "suspends" ethics for a larger purpose. Faith requires a leap into the unknown, a deep attachment to the mystery of Christ, even when to do so contradicts reason. Faith is a movement that leads the believer to renounce everything, including his own intelligence: it was absurd for Abraham to believe that having renounced his own son, his son would be restored to him. Yet Abraham believed in the absurd, and it was by virtue of the absurd that Isaac was restored to him. Kierkegaard became the "religious man" when he broke off his engagement and renounced his youthful ambition to become a pastor. In the religious stage it is no longer a question of devoting oneself to oneself (aesthetic stage) or to others (ethical stage), but of devoting oneself entirely to the transcendent. This relationship to the divine excludes all compromise with society. Only the religious man can live an authentic existence. He is a "knight of the faith." His faith contains no guarantees of certainty and provides little by way of intellectual security. He does not fear the absurd; he hopes against hope.

Kierkegaard does not try to strengthen the believer's certainty: he calls him to plunge headlong into the waters, doubts and all. He rejects as pathological the attitude of seeking guarantees and reasons to believe. Faith cannot be proven. It must be experienced. The Christian is a lover of God. Passion is in no need of justification.

Existential Despair

For Kierkegaard, to be oneself is not to remain trapped in a particular existential state but to move on to the next one.

He asserts that the great instrument of personal growth is not doubt (as with the rationalists) but "despair." In despair, the whole person expresses himself. In doubt, only his reason.

Regarding despair, he believed one must despair of oneself. Despair is not the fear of being nothing: it is the fear of *remaining* nothing. Despair is dynamic and deeply moral. Despair develops our higher powers and moves us from one existential stage to another.

The highest form of despair is repentance, conversion, the transition to the state of religious man.

LIVING ACCORDING TO KIERKEGAARD

To live according to Kierkegaard is to live an authentic life. It is to love oneself, to love one's subjectivity, to love one's singular existence and that of each individual.

To live according to Kierkegaard is to refuse to dissolve into the anonymous Whole. It is to renounce the culturally, religiously, and politically correct.

To live according to Kierkegaard is to affirm the primacy of the individual, to reject all forms of totalitarianism, be they red, black, green, or any other hue.

To live according to Kierkegaard is to make conscious, free, and resolute choices, and to live them so intensely as to experience a vertiginous thrill.

To live according to Kierkegaard is to know how to "despair" of oneself so as to move forward in life, to repent

continued

> LIVING ACCORDING TO KIERKEGAARD *continued*
>
> in order to take the great leap that God expects of each of us, to stop "playing at being a Christian."
>
> To live according to Kierkegaard is to love Jesus Christ not intellectually, but passionately, in the madness of the Cross.

3

THE HUMANITY OF FYODOR DOSTOYEVSKY
(1821–1881)

FYODOR DOSTOYEVSKY WAS BORN in Moscow on November 11, 1821, in the Mariinsky Hospital for the Poor. His father, Mikhail Dostoyevsky, a veteran of the "Patriotic War" of 1812 against Napoleon, was the head doctor at the same hospital. He was an impulsive, suspicious, and sullen man. His wife, Maria Nechayeva, came from a merchant family. Sweet and pious by nature, but in chronic poor health, she was in awe of her husband. Together they had eight children, of whom Fyodor was the second.

In 1827, Mikhail became a "collegiate assessor," a post which made him a member of the nobility by hereditary right. He bought the rural estate of Darovoe in the province of Tula, ninety-three miles south of Moscow. The children spent their summers there exploring the Russian countryside.

Throughout his life, Fyodor had happy memories of his childhood. In *The Brothers Karamazov*, his last novel, he puts words on the lips of the monastic elder, Zosima, that echo his earliest memories of his childhood home:

> From my parents' house I took only good memories. . . . Even from the worst of families, one can keep precious memories, if only one's soul is in search of what is precious. . . . We had a book with beautiful illustrations, entitled *One Hundred and Four Holy Stories from the Old and New Testaments*. It was with this book that I learned to read. I keep it in my library as a wonderful souvenir.[1]

In 1870, Dostoyevsky came across a copy of this same edition and would cherish it for the rest of his life.

Dostoyevsky expresses fond memories of his childhood through the words of Alyosha, the principal character of *The Brothers Karamazov*. Alyosha reminisces in his speech to the classmates of the young Ilyushka whose funeral has just taken place:

> Know that there is nothing higher, stronger, healthier, or more useful for our future life than a good memory, especially a childhood memory from the family home. Know that a beautiful childhood memory, a sacred memory, is perhaps the best thing for our upbringing. If we keep such memories, we are saved for the rest of our lives. Even if we keep in our hearts only one good memory, that can serve at a given moment for our salvation.[2]

---

1. F. Dostoyevsky, *The Brothers Karamazov* (1879–1880), bk. 6, chap. 2.

2. Dostoyevsky, *The Brothers Karamazov*, epilogue, chap. 3.

This speech he wrote became autobiographical: his fond memories of childhood enabled Dostoyevsky to endure facing a firing squad and forced labor.

In 1837, Dostoyevsky's mother died of tuberculosis at the age of thirty-six. Fyodor was sixteen. His father was shattered by her death. He retired, moved to the countryside with his youngest children, and placed the eldest, Mikhail and Fyodor, in the St. Petersburg Military Engineering Academy despite the passion they shared for literature.

Fyodor passed his exams and was admitted to the academy in January 1838. Mikhail was rejected for reasons of health. The two brothers engaged in a prolonged and lively correspondence.

Dostoyevsky, who had no vocation as an engineer, resented studying at the academy. He sensed his untapped creative powers and suffered from not being able to develop them. He devoted all his free time to reading. He gave free rein to his imagination. Gradually, the main theme of his life emerged. He wrote to his brother Mikhail: "Man is a mystery. You must get to the bottom of it, and if you spend a lifetime doing so, don't say you've wasted your time; I'm studying this mystery because I want to be a human being."[3]

In the summer of 1839, Fyodor received a letter from his father announcing his imminent bankruptcy. A few days later, he learned that his father had died: Mikhail was killed by serfs who were outraged by their master's mistreatment. For the rest of his life, Dostoyevsky would

---

3. F. Dostoyevsky, Letter to Mikhail, August 16, 1839.

not believe this version of events: the image of the brutal landlord contradicted the good opinion he had of his father. And with good reason: on June 18, 1975, an article appeared in *Literaturnaya Gazeta* entitled "Speculation and the Logic of Facts" in which the Soviet historian German Fyodorov showed, based on archival documents, that Mikhail Dostoyevsky had died of a stroke.

Upon graduating from the academy in 1843, Fyodor was given the rank of second lieutenant and joined the field planning section of the St. Petersburg Engineering Department as a draftsman. The job bored him to tears.

Soon a profound change took place in Fyodor's soul. The man who had only recently been dreaming of fantastic adventures in the style of Walter Scott was now writing a book—*Poor Folk*—which told the story of a shy, elderly, miserable civil servant in St. Petersburg. In it, the exotic, the heroic, the romantic, the mysterious, and the extraordinary give way to everything that is most commonplace. In the "fantastic" city of St. Petersburg, Dostoyevsky understood that there is nothing more "fantastic" than reality.

In a short story from 1861 entitled *Petersburg Visions in Prose and Verse*, Fyodor recounts his "vision on the Neva":

> It was as if I understood at that moment that thing which until now had only stirred within me; as if I were entering a new world, a world which I knew only by obscure rumors, mysterious signs. I believe that it was at this precise moment that I began to live. . . . Tell me, gentlemen, am I not a fantasist, have I not been

a mystic since my early childhood? What happened? Nothing, absolutely nothing, just a feeling.[4]

Gogol, the author of "The Overcoat" (a short story published in 1843, also about the misadventures of a minor official in Petersburg), was the great inspiration for this change. Gogol extracts the extraordinary (the absurd, the demented, the repulsive) from the ordinary. The philosopher Nikolai Berdyaev writes:

> Dostoyevsky is inspired by Gogol, especially in his early novels. In Dostoyevsky, however, the approach to man is quite different. Gogol's man is a being in a state of decomposition; there are no human beings in his works, only strange faces. . . . Dostoyevsky, on the other hand, discovers the greatness of man even in the most fallen creature.[5]

In 1844, less than a year before leaving the army, Fyodor completed the first Russian translation of Balzac's *Eugenie Grandet*, was subsequently would be published without mentioning his name as translator. He learned the technique of the novel from the French writer.

The text of *Poor Folk*, which he rewrote four times out of a desire for perfection, was completed in 1845. On the advice of his friend and roommate at the time, the writer Dmitri Grigorovich, Dostoyevsky presented his

---

4. F. Dostoyevsky, *Petersburg Visions in Prose and Verse* (1861).

5. N. Berdiaev, Н. А. Бердяев, Миросозерцание Достоевского [Dostoyevsky's vision of the world*] (1923), chap. 1, translation from Russian.

manuscript to the poet Nikolai Nekrasov. In his book *The Russian Novel*, Eugène-Melchior de Vogüé recounts:

> At three o'clock in the morning, Dostoyevsky heard a knock at his door: it was Grigorovich returning, bringing Nekrasov. The poet rushed into the stranger's arms with heightened emotion; he had been reading the novel all night, and his soul was overwhelmed. . . . On leaving his new protégé, Nekrasov went straight to Belinsky, the oracle of Russian thought, the critic whose very name made literary novices quake. "A new Gogol has been born to us!" the poet exclaimed as he entered his friend's house. "Gogols are growing like mushrooms today," replied the critic in his most caustic manner; and he took the manuscript as he would a crust of poisoned bread. But its effect on Belinsky too was magical.[6]

Dostoyevsky was warmly welcomed into Vassarion Belinsky's circle and became famous even before Nekrasov published his novel in January 1846. Years later, in his *Writer's Diary*, Dostoyevsky reported Belinsky's words from their first meeting: "Do you understand, young man, the whole truth about what you have written? . . . It is the revelation of art, a gift from above: respect this gift and you will be a great writer!" And Dostoyevsky comments: "It was the most delicious moment of my life. In prison, when I remembered those words, I regained my courage."[7]

---

6. E. de Vogüé, *Le Roman russe* [The Russian novelists] (Paris: E. Plon, Nourrit et Cie, 1924), p. 120.

7. F. Dostoyevsky, *Writer's Diary*, January 1877.

His next work, *The Double*, was met with total incomprehension. The previous enthusiastic recognition of his genius gave way to the most profound disappointment. Belinsky kept his distance.

In the spring of 1846, the writer Alexei Pleshcheev introduced Dostoyevsky to the Russian Fourierist,[8] Mikhail Petrachevsky. Within Petrachevsky's circle, Dostoyevsky became close to Nikolai Spechnev, who claimed to be a communist. In the spring of 1849, Sergei Durov created a smaller circle—in effect, a secret, underground society—which was joined by the most radical members of Petrachevsky's circle, including Dostoyevsky, Pleshcheev, and Spechnev. Their aim was to set up a clandestine printing house and to organize a *coup d'état*.

At meetings of the Durov circle, Dostoyevsky repeatedly read out Belinsky's Letter to Gogol of 15 July 1847. In this "forbidden" letter (so called because the government had censored it), Belinsky, under the influence of Feuerbach, railed against Gogol's religiosity:

> What Russia needs is not sermons (she has heard enough of them!) or prayers (she has repeated them too often!), but the awakening in the people of a sense of their human dignity lost for so many centuries amid dirt and refuse; she needs rights and laws conforming not to the preaching of the church but to common sense and justice, and their strictest possible observance. Instead of which she presents the dire spectacle . . . of a country where not only are the rights of

---

8. Charles Fourier (1772–1837) was a French utopian socialist.

the person, rights to honor and property not defended, but where huge corporations of thieves and robbers—all official—take the place of the police. . . . Look closer, and you will see that the Russian people are by nature a deeply atheistic people.[9]

Dostoyevsky found Belinsky's teaching fascinating. The faith of his childhood proved fragile. The religious question was absent from the works he published before his arrest.

"I could probably never have become a Nechaev," Dostoyevsky said years later, "but a Nechaevian, perhaps, . . . in my youth."[10] Sergei Nechaev was the founder of a revolutionary society in the 1860s and the author of the *Revolutionary Catechism*. He dreamed of establishing a network of secret cells throughout Russia with the aim of stirring up the masses, overthrowing the government, and destroying religion, family, and property. Durov's revolutionary cell, with its secret printing press and insurrectionary program, closely resembled a Nechaevian organization. In *The Devils,* Dostoyevsky would portray the demons of the future Russian revolution with striking realism, having been one of them himself.

Spechnev, the central figure in the Durov circle, exerted enormous influence on Dostoyevsky. A handsome man from a wealthy family, his striking good looks easily attracted attention. At one time, he had an affair with a

---

9. V. G. Belinsky, Письмо к Гоголю [Letter to Gogol*], ed/ N. F. Belchikov (Moscow: State Publishing House, 1936), http://az.lib.ru/b/belinskij_w_g/text_3890.shtml, translated from Russian.

10. Belinsky.

certain Anna Savelieva, a landowner, who abandoned her husband and two children to go abroad with him. There, she committed suicide. Back in Russia, Spechnev preached socialism, atheism, and terrorism. He was one of the first readers in Russia of the *Manifesto of the Communist Party* (1848) by Karl Marx and Friedrich Engels.

Spechnev was more prone to listen than to talk. Although capable of charm and a show of affability, he was, by nature, cold and reserved. As a Communist, he disliked the idle chatter of the liberals in Petrachevsky's circle. Very likely it was Spechnev who brought the extremist Durov circle into being. Attractive and yet ice cold, charismatic and yet mysterious, Spechnev, for all his contradictions, won Dostoyevsky's unalloyed devotion. He felt this strange man's charm as well as his demonic power. Dostoyevsky would immortalize him a few decades later in the person of Nikolai Stavrogin, the central character of his prophetic *The Devils*.

On the morning of April 23, 1849, shortly after the publication of Dostoyevsky's short story *White Nights*, the writer and the other members of Petrachevsky's circle were arrested and detained in the Peter and Paul Fortress. For having read Belinsky's letter in public and failing to report its distribution, Dostoyevsky was sentenced to death by firing squad. A week later, the sentence was commuted to eight years of hard labor. Tsar Nicholas I reduced the sentence to four years but added a year of compulsory military service as a common soldier. The tsar decided not to inform the prisoners that their death sentences had been commuted until they were facing the firing squad and the soldiers were on the point of pulling the trigger. As this macabre pantomime was being played out, one of the condemned, Nikolai Grigoriev, went mad and never regained his sanity.

"After they read us the death sentence," Dostoyevsky wrote to his brother Mikhail,

> we were told to kiss the cross, our swords were broken over our heads, and we were handed white shirts—the costume of those condemned to death. Then three were tied to the pillar for execution. I was the sixth. Three at a time were called out; consequently, I was in the second batch and had no more than a minute left to live. I remembered you, brother, and all of you; during the last minute, I thought only of you; only then did I realize how much I loved you, my dear brother! I also managed to embrace Pleshcheyev and Durov, who were at either side of me, and say goodbye to them. Finally, the execution was cancelled, the men were untied from their pillars, and it was announced that His Imperial Majesty had spared our lives.[11]

We know how Dostoyevsky felt at the point of execution when we read one of Prince Myshkin's monologues in *The Idiot*. Facing imminent death, Dostoyevsky felt "the gift of life." Prince Myshkin in *The Idiot*, Makar Dolgoruky in *The Adolescent*, Elder Zosima in *The Brothers Karamazov*, all speak of this gift of life which is at the very heart of the mystery of existence.

---

11. F. Dostoyevsky, Letter to Mikhail, December 22, 1849.

In Tobolsk, Western Siberia, during the convicts' journey to the penal colony, the wives of the exiled Decembrists (participants in the failed military coup of December 1825) organized a meeting of all the deported members of Petrachevsky's group. They gave each of them a Bible with a few rubles concealed in the binding. Dostoyevsky kept his Bible as a relic for the rest of his life.

On January 23, 1850, Fyodor arrived at the Omsk penitentiary. To his brother Andrei he would later write: "During those four years, it was as if I had been buried alive and sealed in a coffin. It was unspeakable, endless suffering. Every hour, every minute weighed on my soul like a stone."[12]

The years in prison marked a definitive turning point in the writer's spiritual evolution. In *The House of the Dead*, a largely autobiographical work on which Dostoyevsky had been working since his release from prison, the narrator recalls:

> For all those years, among the crowd of inmates, I was in total solitude, a solitude which I came to love. I reconsidered the whole of my past life, I picked over everything down to the smallest detail, I pondered my past deeply and judged myself sternly and implacably. At times I even thanked fate for sending me this time of isolation, without which neither this judgment of myself nor this strict revision of my former life would have taken place. And what hope I had in my heart at such moments! I thought, I resolved, I vowed to myself

---

12. F. Dostoyevsky, Letter to Andrei, November 6, 1854.

that in my future life there would be no more mistakes, no more failures. . . . I was waiting for freedom, I was calling for it with all my being, I wanted to prove myself again in a new struggle.[13]

It would be too simplistic to think that during his years in prison Dostoyevsky became a believer. What is certain, however, is that he came out with a deep thirst for belief.

Dostoyevsky was sent as a common infantryman to Semipalatinsk, Siberia, where he befriended Maria Isayeva. Her husband, Alexander Isaev, was a local official and a man with a noble heart. But he was also an inveterate drunkard. He died a few months later.

In the hope of obtaining a full pardon from Tsar Alexander II (who succeeded Nicholas I), Dostoyevsky asked Adjutant General Edward Totleben, an old acquaintance of his and a hero of the Crimean War, to intercede with the tsar on his behalf. On August 26, 1856, the day of Alexander II's coronation, Alexander pardoned the former members of Petrachevsky's group, but ordered that Dostoyevsky be secretly monitored until his reliability was fully established.

Dostoyevsky married Maria Isayeva, and in 1859 returned to St. Petersburg with Maria and Pavel, her son by her late husband. Their conjugal life did not come close to the romantic vision he had built up of it. The marriage was a complete failure.

In 1860, Dostoyevsky penned his prison memoir, *The House of the Dead*, becoming the first writer to tackle the

---

13. F. Dostoyevsky, *The House of the Dead* (1862), chap. 9.

subject of convict life. It was a great success and remains a landmark in the history of prison camp literature.

In 1862, for the first time, Dostoyevsky traveled abroad. He visited Germany, France, England, Switzerland, Italy, and Austria. In the German spa town of Baden-Baden, where he intended to take the waters, he began frequenting the casinos, became addicted to gambling, and soon fell into debt.

In 1863, as his wife lay dying, he made a second trip to Europe, part of it in the company of a certain Apollinaria Suslova, an "emancipated" young woman, whom he would meet again in 1865 in Wiesbaden. Both Dostoyevsky's gambling addiction and his complex relationship with Suslova ("an infernal woman," in his words) would find literary expression in *The Gambler*.

Notes from Underground (1864) marks a new stage in the development of Dostoyevsky's talent. In it, the man in the cellar is not a revolutionary: he is a man without a will, crushed by the awareness of evil in the world and his powerlessness to remedy it. This powerlessness turns his love of humanity into hatred. Dostoyevsky grasped the moral tragedy that awaited him if he persisted in living in a world without God.

In 1864, Dostoyevsky's wife, Maria, and his elder brother, Mikhail, died. In February 1865, six months after the latter's death, the magazine *Epoch*, which the Dostoyevsky brothers had founded jointly in 1863, ceased publication. Having assumed responsibility for the magazine's debts, Dostoyevsky was forced to accept a contract with the publishing house of Fyodor Stellovsky to publish all of his previous works. The terms of the contract were harsh for the writer.

The first chapters of *Crime and Punishment* were published in early 1866 in the magazine *Russkiy Vestnik* (*The Russian Messenger*). But the contract with Stellovsky required Dostoyevsky to send him the manuscript of a hitherto unpublished novel (it was to be *The Gambler*) by November 1, 1866. This delayed the completion of *Crime and Punishment*. Dostoyevsky's friend Alexander Miliukov found the best stenographer in St. Petersburg, Anna Snitkina, to speed up the writing of *The Gambler*. After handing over the manuscript to the publisher, Dostoyevsky proposed marriage to the stenographer. On February 15, 1867, they married in the Cathedral of the Holy Trinity. They would have four children together. It was probably during his marriage to Snitkina that Dostoyevsky finally converted to Christianity.

The income he derived from *Crime and Punishment* was not negligible. To prevent it from being seized by creditors, he fled to Europe with Anna and remained there for four years.

Dostoyevsky returned to St. Petersburg in 1871, initiating one of the happiest and most fruitful periods of his life. Anna took care of the finances and Fyodor gave up gambling for good.

In 1878, Aleksei Dostoyevsky, their beloved son, died of an epileptic fit at the age of three. The event left the writer deeply shaken.

Among Dostoyevsky's most important writings are *The Diary of a Writer* (1873–1881), a philosophical, literary, and journalistic work; and five novels: *Crime and Punishment* (1866), *The Idiot* (1868), *The Devils* (1871–1872), *The Adolescent* (1875), and *The Brothers Karamazov* (1879–1880).

On June 8, 1880, speaking before the Society of Lovers of Russian Literature at the dedication of the monument to Aleksandr Pushkin in central Moscow, delivered an oration on Pushkin's greatness that is remembered to this day. He noted Pushkin's ability to embody the "genius" of other nations and cultures, so much so that in *Don Juan*, Pushkin "is" a Spaniard; in *A Feast in Time of Plague*, an Englishman; in *Imitations of the Koran,* an Arab; in *Egyptian Nights*, a Roman. He concluded:

> Yes, beyond all doubt, the destiny of a Russian is pan-European and universal. To become a true Russian, to become fully Russian (and you should remember this), means to become the brother of all men, to become, if you will, *a universal man.* . . . Pushkin died in the full maturity of his powers, and undeniably bore away with him a great secret into the grave. And now we, without him, are seeking to divine his secret.[14]

During the night of January 25, 1881, he coughed up blood and lost consciousness. When he revived, he said to his wife, "Anya, send for a priest immediately, I want to confess and receive Communion." Very early in the morning of January 28, he confided to her: "You know,

---

14. F. Dostoyevsky, Speech before the Society of Lovers of Russian Literature, June 8, 1880.

Anya, I haven't slept for three hours. I'm going to die today." Anna reassured her husband, but he interrupted her: "No, I know I'm going to die today. Light a candle, Anya, and give me the Gospel."[15]

Lyubov, the writer's daughter, states in her memoirs that her father, as he lay dying, called her and her brother and asked them to read the parable of the Prodigal Son. He then said to them:

> My children, never forget what you have just heard here. Keep your faith in the Lord and never despair of his forgiveness. I love you very much, but my love is nothing compared to God's infinite love for all people. Even if you commit a crime in your life, do not lose hope in the Lord. You are his children, humble yourselves before him as before your father, ask him for forgiveness, and he will rejoice in your repentance as He rejoiced in the return of the prodigal son.[16]

Shortly before seven o'clock at night, Dostoyevsky expired.

Dostoyevsky did not study philosophy; he did not write philosophical treatises and he never claimed to be a philosopher. His contemporaries did not consider his

---

15. "Читайте Достоевского, любите Достоевского" ["Read Dostoyevsky, love Dostoyevsky"*], Казанский федеральный университет, February 9, 2015, https://kpfu.ru/mediacenter/gazeta-39kazanskij-universitet39/chitajte-dostoevskogo-ljubite-dostoevskogo-113416.html, translation from Russian.

16. L. Dostoyevsky, *Л.Достоевская*. Достоевский в изображении своей дочери [Dostoyevsky as portrayed by his daughter*] (1920), p. 162, translation from Russian.

writings to be philosophical. Dostoyevsky is, however, one of the most *philosophical* writers who ever lived. If there are few men of science who have done as much for philosophy as Pascal, there are few men of letters who have done as much for philosophy as Dostoyevsky.

"The whole of Dostoyevsky's work," writes Berdyaev,

> is the artistic embodiment and tragic movement of ideas. The hero of the *Underground* is an idea, Raskolnikov is an idea, Stavrogin, Kirilov, Shatov, Pyotr Verkhovensky are ideas, Ivan Karamazov is an idea. All of Dostoyevsky's heroes are absorbed by an idea, intoxicated by an idea; ideas, in the Platonic sense of the term, obsess Dostoyevsky. . . . Dostoyevsky said of himself: "I am weak in philosophy, but I am strongly in love with it." He was not strong in academic philosophy, but his intuitive genius allowed him to philosophize in another way. He was a true philosopher, one of the greatest Russian philosophers. . . . Dostoyevsky's work is of radical importance for philosophical anthropology, for the philosophy of history, for the philosophy of religion, for moral philosophy.[17]

Dostoyevsky's Personality

"Dostoyevsky has a passionate desire to love and be loved," writes the philosopher Nicholas Lossky.

> He defines himself as "a man with a tender heart, who does not know how to communicate his feelings." He

---

17. Berdiaev, Н. А. Бердяев, Миросозерцание Достоевского [Dostoyevsky's vision of the world*], chap. 1.

constantly complains about his repugnant character: "Sometimes I am unable to utter a single kind word, even though my heart is full of love." It is therefore not surprising that he satisfies his thirst for love in his dreams and pours it out in short stories, such as "White Nights," "Netochka Nezvanova," "The Landlady," "Poor Folk," "A Little Hero." . . . When circumstances, family ties or simply habit make the obstacles between Dostoyevsky and others disappear, the tenderness of his soul and his goodness are revealed with strength and clarity. . . . Many are the facts that testify to his extraordinary goodness.[18]

Dostoyevsky was deeply melancholic by nature: he lived inside himself. In 1847, in a letter to his brother Mikhail, he admitted to suffering from a psychological imbalance: "When the exterior life is lacking, the interior life takes over dangerously. Nerves and fantasy then occupy a predominant place. The smallest external event then seems colossal and frightening. You begin to fear life."[19] Dostoyevsky was often on the verge of madness. His creative writing saved him, offering an escape from the unbearable tension between the exterior and the interior.

In Dostoyevsky's works we discover his hidden struggles, his intimate conflicts. The analysis of his work allows us to reconstruct his personality in all its psychological and spiritual complexity. In his novels, the saints and sinners are himself. "In the lives of his characters, it is his life that he

---

18. N. Lossky, Н.О. Лосский, Достоевский [Dostoyevsky and his christian worldview*], vol. 1, p. 1, translation from Russian.

19. F. Dostoyevsky, Letter to Mikhail, January–February 1847.

recounts, in their doubts it is his doubts that he expresses, in their faults it is his faults that he discovers, in the contradictions of their behavior, his contradictions, in their crimes, the secret crimes that he commits in his heart."[20]

Dostoyevsky was a deeply contradictory personality. His noble ideals coexisted with vice: vanity (his literary success often turned his head), intemperance (at the roulette wheel and the debauchery that that implies), and above all injustice. Dostoyevsky was unfair to his first wife, Maria: a year and a half before her death, when she was suffering from tuberculosis, Dostoyevsky cheated on her with Suslova. He was unfair to the Poles, the Jews, the Germans, the English, and the French, whom he constantly insulted in his *Diary*, although he deeply loved the great culture of Western Europe. He was unfair to his people: he so deified the relationship between the Russian *muzhik* (peasant) and the tsar that he unconsciously favored the rise of the sinister Rasputin: "It was Grigory Rasputin who killed the monarchy," says Berdyaev. "The link between the Tsar and Rasputin mystically completed the autocracy. . . . It was the punishment of Russian populism, which made the pagan national element a god separate from the universal Logos, the universal Church."[21]

In Dostoyevsky, every sort of misery coexisted with his nobility of soul. In this respect he differed greatly

---

20. Berdiaev, Н. А. Бердяев, Миросозерцание Достоевского [Dostoyevsky's vision of the world*], chap. 1.

21. N. Berdiaev, Н.А. Бердяев, Духовные основы русской революции. Опыты 1917—1918 гг. СПб.: РХГИ, 1999. С. 15–16 [The spiritual foundations of the Russian Revolution*], translation from Russian.

from Pascal and Soloviev, in whom the desire for moral excellence and sanctity was much more pronounced.

"I Want To Be a Human Being"

At eighteen, Dostoyevsky had already discovered and formulated his vital mission: "Man is a mystery. You must get to the bottom of it. . . . I'm studying this mystery because I want to be a human being."[22]

At the age of twenty-nine, when he was about to leave for prison, he said goodbye to Mikhail:

> Brother, I'm not depressed and haven't lost heart. Everywhere life is life. . . . To be a human being among human beings, and to remain so, even in misfortune, without becoming discouraged and without falling—this is what life is, therein lies its meaning.[23]

"Dostoyevsky is obsessed with man," writes Berdyaev.[24] "The exterior—the city with its peculiar atmosphere, the flats with their awful furniture, the inns with their execrable stench—are only signs, symbols of the inner world of man, reflections of his spiritual journey."[25]

Unlike Tolstoy, Dostoyevsky is not a psychologist. He is an anthropologist. His science is that of philosophical and theological anthropology. "Dostoyevsky takes

---

22. Dostoyevsky, Letter to Mikhail, August 16, 1839.

23. Dostoyevsky, Letter to Mikhail, December 22, 1849.

24. Berdiaev, Н. А. Бердяев, Миросозерцание Достоевского [Dostoyevsky's vision of the world*], chap. 2.

25. Berdiaev, Н. А. Бердяев, Миросозерцание Достоевского [Dostoyevsky's vision of the world*], chap. 1.

us out of the closed circle of psychologism and into the eternal questions. He knows that the dignity of man is revealed in its fullness not in the psychological sphere, but in the spiritual and religious sphere."[26]

Dostoyevsky is imbued with a boundless compassion for man, although he is far from being a sentimental humanist. He preaches compassion but also suffering. He demands suffering because he believes in its redemptive power.

Love and compassion for man, the defense of his dignity and freedom, the search for the face of God in man, the thirst for purifying pain—this is Dostoyevsky.

"Man Is Broad . . ."

"Beauty is a terrible and awful thing!" declares Dmitri Karamazov.

> I can't endure the thought that a man of lofty mind and heart begins with the ideal of the Madonna and ends with the ideal of Sodom. What's still more awful is that a man with the ideal of Sodom in his soul does not renounce the ideal of the Madonna, and his heart may be on fire with that ideal, genuinely on fire, just as in his days of youth and innocence. Yes, man is broad, too broad, indeed. I'd have him narrower. . . . God and the devil are fighting there, and the battlefield is the heart of man.[27]

---

26. Berdiaev, Н. А. Бердяев, Миросозерцание Достоевского [Dostoyevsky's vision of the world*], chap. 1.

27. Dostoyevsky, *The Brothers Karamazov*, bk. 3, chap. 3.

Man is broad, the human spirit is vast in its propensity for good and evil. In prison, Dostoyevsky rubbed elbows with prisoners who were incapable of showing the slightest repentance for their infamous crimes. He was confronted with the real power of evil, the demonic power of sin. His "naturalistic" convictions (his initial Rousseauian faith in the absolute goodness of man) collapsed one after the other like a house of cards. He realized that alongside the sociopolitical evil he fought against in his youth, there was a deeper, more fundamental, more dangerous personal evil. Rousseauism, liberalism, socialism, all those doctrines that deny the existence of original sin, fall to pieces.

Dostoyevsky rebelled against the sociological explanation of evil, against the denial of freedom and personal responsibility. If man is only a product of his environment, he surmised, then he is nothing. This reduction of man to matter aroused the writer's anger.

Dostoyevsky was aware of the power of evil, but he kept his faith in man's freedom and personal responsibility. Man is broad in his freedom and responsibility, he believed. Man is not "too broad," and only the Antichrist can feel the desire "to have him narrower."

God Made Man

Dostoyevsky believed in man because he believed God became man. Even in his tragic fall, man discovers the radiant face of Christ, his humanity, and his mercy. He regains confidence in himself, purifies and saves himself through suffering and penance.

"Faith in man," writes Berdyaev, "is faith in Jesus Christ, the God who became man. . . . In the name of Christ, in the name of the infinite love he feels for Christ, Dostoyevsky breaks with the atheistic humanism of which Belinsky is the prophet."[28]

It was within the walls of the Peter and Paul Fortress that Dostoyevsky's long process of conversion began at the age of twenty-nine. When he left the penal colony four years later, he noted how far he had come: "In the colony I understood myself . . . , I understood Christ . . . , I understood Russian man."[29]

Dostoyevsky was captivated by the humanity of Christ, by his perfect human nature, by the extent of his natural virtues. On leaving the penitentiary, he wrote to Natalia Fonvizina, one of the women who offered a Bible to each member of Petrachevsky's circle:

> I will tell you that I am a child of this century, a child of disbelief and doubt. I am that today and will remain so until the grave. How much terrible torture this thirst for faith has cost me and costs me even now, which is all the stronger in my soul the more arguments I can find against it. And yet, God sends

---

28. Berdiaev, Н. А. Бердяев, Миросозерцание Достоевского [Dostoyevsky's vision of the world*], chap. 1.

29. V. Soloviev, Вс. Соловьёв, Воспоминания о Ф.М. Достоевском, Исторический вестник [Recollections of F. Dostoyevsky, *Historical Bulletin* 3 (1881)]; translation from Russian.

me sometimes moments when I am completely calm; at those moments I love and feel loved by others, and it is at those moments that I have shaped for myself a Credo where everything is clear and sacred for me. This Credo is very simple, here it is: to believe that nothing is more beautiful, profound, sympathetic, reasonable, manly and more powerful than Christ. . . . Even if someone were to prove to me that the truth lay outside Christ, I should prefer to remain with Christ than with the truth.[30]

Dostoyevsky had no use for a divinity that has not become man, nor for a Truth that has not become flesh. He accepted the divinity of Christ because he was in love with his humanity.

The Man-God Versus the God-Man

In *The Devils*, Kirilov announces the reign of the man-god. "The God-man?" asks Stavrogin. "The man-god!" replies Kirilov, "that's the whole difference."[31] Modern man rejects God and with him the reality of the God-man. Consciously or unconsciously, he creates the conditions for the appearance of the man-god. "If God does not exist," says Kirilov, "then I am God."[32] The man-god is the one for whom everything is permitted.

---

30. F. Dostoyevsky, Letter to N. Fonvizina, Omsk, 1854.
31. F. Dostoyevsky, *The Devils*, part 2, chap. 5.
32. Dostoyevsky, *The Devils*, part 6, chap. 2.

Raskolnikov, the central character in *Crime and Punishment*, would have liked to be the man-god. He is greedy for power, he seeks to "dominate the trembling creatures, to dominate the whole anthill." He asks himself, "Am I a louse like everybody else or a man? . . . Am I a trembling creature or do I have the *right*?"[33] In murdering the old woman, he wants to prove to himself that he is neither a "louse" nor a "trembling creature." He kills her, but the doubts that assail him afterward show his "weakness." "I did not know how to make the leap. I fell short, I only knew how to kill," he tells Sonia.

> The devil led me on then and he has shown me since that I had not the right to take that path, because I am just such a louse as all the rest. He was mocking me and here I've come to you now! Welcome your guest! If I were not a louse, should I have come to you? Listen: when I went then to the old woman's I only went to try. . . . You may be sure of that![34]

Raskolnikov is a "failure," a louse, a trembling creature, unable to cross the line beyond which man becomes God. He still carries the "burden" of his conscience. Guilt gnaws at him to such an extent that he thinks of committing suicide several times and finally turns himself in to the police because he is a coward and a fool.

Pyotr Verkhovensky in *The Devils*—unlike Raskolnikov—embodies the man-god. For Dostoyevsky, the reign of the man-god is the reign of the approaching revolution:

---

33. Dostoyevsky, *The Devils*, part 5, chap. 4.
34. Dostoyevsky, *The Devils*, part 5, chap. 4.

"Listen. We are going to make a revolution," Pyotr Verkhovensky muttered rapidly, almost deliriously. . . . "We are going to make such an upheaval as to rock the whole order of things to its foundation. . . . Every member of society keeps an eye on the other, and it's his duty to inform. Everyone belongs to all and all to everyone. . . . Equality must reign in a herd. . . . We will smother the geniuses in their cradles. . . . Slaves must have masters. . . . Absolute obedience, absolute impersonality, but once every thirty years, they will all suddenly begin eating each other up . . . for the sole purpose of not getting bored. . . . Everywhere a measureless vanity, a bestial appetite without precedent. . . . Unparalleled debauchery, vile, filthy. . . . It will be an upheaval such as the world has never seen before. In this there will be a force, an incredible force! All we need is a lever to lift the earth. Everything will rise up. And the sea will rise, and the whole flimsy structure will fall to the ground and then we shall consider how to build up an edifice of stone. For the first time! It is *we* who are going to build it, we, and only we!"[35]

The man-god does not hesitate. He has no doubts or remorse. He has the power to do anything, even the unimaginable. Just ten years after the release of *The Devils*, Nietzsche, in his *Zarathustra*, elaborated the figure of the superman, whose fundamental features strikingly resemble those of Dostoyevsky's man-god.

---

35. Dostoyevsky, *The Devils*, part 2, chap. 8.

The "Grand Inquisitor": The Failure of Atheistic Humanism

The pinnacle of Dostoyevsky's work is "The Legend of the Grand Inquisitor" in *The Brothers Karamazov*. It is arguably one of the most brilliant works of world literature, and its philosophical depth is no less remarkable.

The story, which Ivan Karamazov composed and tells his brother Alyosha, takes place in fifteenth-century Seville. Ivan imagines that Jesus has returned to earth to take a closer look at the Spanish Inquisition—an episode in history which can hardly be said to have conformed to Christ's teaching. The Grand Inquisitor claps him in chains and condemns him to death:

> "Tomorrow, I will burn you at the stake. . . . Was it not you who said so often at that time, 'I want to set you free'? Well, you have seen them today, those 'free' men. . . . Yes, that affair cost us very dearly . . . , but, we finally closed it. . . . For fifteen centuries we tortured ourselves with this freedom, but now it is over, and well over. . . . Know that it is now, yes, at this very moment, when these people have freely offered us their freedom and slavishly set it at our feet, that they are surer than ever of being fully free. . . . Nothing, ever, either for human society or man, has been more unbearable than freedom! . . . They know that they can never be free because they are weak, vicious, rebellious. . . . But he alone can take over the freedom of men who appeases their conscience. . . ."

> The Inquisitor remains silent; he waits for his prisoner to respond. His silence oppresses him. He saw that the prisoner listened in a subdued and earnest manner looking him straight in the eye, without wanting to say anything in reply. The old man wanted him to say something, even something dreadful or embittered. But He suddenly approaches the old man, and, without saying anything kisses his bloodless, ninety-year-old lips. That is his whole answer. The old man shudders. . . . The kiss scalded his heart.[36]

The Grand Inquisitor is a tragic figure. He gave his life in the service of Christ, but toward the end of his days he lost his faith. He accuses Christ of having overestimated man's abilities and thus made him miserable. The Grand Inquisitor rages against Christ in the name of Christ's own commandment to love one's neighbor. The Grand Inquisitor satanically violates the commandment to love God but fanatically demands the observance of the commandment to love one's neighbor. For the Grand Inquisitor, to love one's neighbor means to "free" him from the unbearable burden of conscience, dignity, freedom, and responsibility. It is to free him, in a word, from his humanity, from all that is human in him!

The Grand Inquisitor is indignant about the elitism of the religion of Christ: "Would you only cherish the tens of thousands of the great and strong, while the vast multitude, who are weak but love you, must exist only

---

36. Dostoyevsky, *The Brothers Karamazov,* bk. 5, chap. 5.

for the sake of the great and strong? No, we cherish the weak, too."[37]

After losing faith in God, the Inquisitor irretrievably loses faith in man. He demands nothing from him and justifies all his sins. In order to make mankind happy—for he is a philanthropist—he has taken away all of its humanity. He loves mankind as one loves one's pet. His love for humanity is a masquerade.

The legend of the Grand Inquisitor is a damning critique of atheistic humanism—if one does not believe in God and the immortality of the soul, the only way to love humanity is to turn it into a bovine herd; the only way to love the world is to turn it into a feedlot farm.

If the "devils," for whom everything is permitted, are the prototypes of the Nietzschean superman who has no other objective than to attain and wield power, the "Grand Inquisitor" of Ivan Karamazov is animated by "good" intentions. He has the appearance of goodness, he seduces. Unlike the "devils," The "Grand Inquisitor" is not cynical. He is hypocritical: in the name of love, he scorns love; in the name of humanity, he corrupts humanity. He is the Antichrist, the counterfeit Christ, the one who comes in his guise to "correct" his work.

Through this legend, Dostoyevsky can finally express what he has been writing about all his life: our freedom cannot be detached from faith in God; freedom is only the image of God in us. In the absence of faith in God, there is only despotism and slavery in the kingdom of the Antichrist.

---

37. Dostoyevsky, *The Brothers Karamazov*, bk. 5, chap. 5.

As Alyosha points out to Ivan, his "poem is in praise of Jesus, it is not a rebuke of Him."[38] Christ's silence, the kiss he plants on the dead lips of the Grand Inquisitor are his—Christ's—glorification. Christ is the liberator of man. Christianity is the religion of spiritual freedom.

> **LIVING ACCORDING TO DOSTOYEVSKY**
>
> To live according to Dostoyevsky is to discover in our personal downfalls the face of Christ—radiant, merciful, deeply human—to discover our dignity, to purify and save ourselves through suffering and penance.
>
> To live according to Dostoyevsky is to have a measureless passion for man, his dignity, his freedom, and his immortal soul. It means wanting to safeguard this dignity in a world that scorns it.
>
> To live according to Dostoyevsky is to affirm freedom as the image of God in man. It is to refuse to give up our freedom in exchange for security and material comfort. It is to refuse to be part of the herd.
>
> To live according to Dostoyevsky is to discover the spirit of the Grand Inquisitor in those who, while claiming to love man and his weakness, justify every kind of sin and thus render superfluous the forgiveness and mercy of God.

---

38. Dostoyevsky, *The Brothers Karamazov*, bk. 5, chap. 5.

4

THE UNIFIED LIFE OF VLADIMIR SOLOVIEV
(1853–1900)

VLADIMIR SOLOVIEV WAS BORN in Moscow on January 28, 1853. His father, Sergei, was one of the most famous Russian historians. Polyxena, his mother, belonged to the old Romanov family, which was of Polish and Cossack origin; her ancestors included the famous Russian-Ukrainian philosopher Grigori Skovoroda, the "first philosopher of the Russian Empire," as he is often called.

Sergei and Polyxena had twelve children, of whom Vladimir was the fourth. Four of their children died in infancy.

One day, when Vladimir was eight years old, his grandfather, Mikhail Soloviev, an Orthodox priest, brought him to the choir of his church and invited him to kneel at the altar. He blessed him and asked God to take him into his service. Mikhail died a few months later. Vladimir would dedicate his treatise on moral philosophy—*The Justification of the Good*—to him.

The young Vladimir had the piety of his grandfather, the intelligence and strength of will of his father, and the deep sensitivity of his mother.

At the age of thirteen, Soloviev abandoned the religion of his childhood. "My free and autonomous intellectual evolution," he wrote,

> began in my thirteenth year with religious skepticism. My spiritual journey was unhappy but coherent. Over a period of four years, I experienced all the phases of European thought of the last four centuries: doubts about the necessity of external manifestations of religiosity, iconoclasm, rationalism, the rejection of miracles and of the divinity of Christ. I was a deist, then a pantheist, and finally an atheist and materialist. At each of these stages I paused for a long time and gave way to passion and fanaticism.[1]

At the age of sixteen, Soloviev finished high school with highest honors. According to his father's wishes, he enrolled in the history faculty of Moscow University, but soon asked to be transferred to the natural sciences section of the physics and mathematics faculty.

"I began my university years with a deeply negative view of religion," he wrote. "I was looking for something new. What interested me in the natural sciences to which I thought I would devote myself was their philosophical scope, not their practical content."[2]

---

1. S. Soloviev, С. Соловьёв, *Жизнь и творческая эволюция Владимира Соловьёва*, стр. 58 (*Vladimir Solovyov: His Life and Creative Evolution*) (1977), p. 58, translation from the Russian.

2. Soloviev, С. Соловьёв, *Жизнь и творческая эволюция Владимира Соловьёва*, стр. 90 (*Vladimir Solovyov: His Life and Creative Evolution*) (1977), p. 90.

During his early years at the university, Soloviev became fascinated with the ideas of Schopenhauer. He accepted his boundless pessimism (the world is ruled by a terrifying and arbitrary will) and his hope of overcoming suffering through nirvana. Schopenhauer's asceticism was for Soloviev a preparation for the asceticism of the gospel.

After studying natural sciences for three years, he left the faculty of physics and mathematics to return to the faculty of history as an auditor. It was at this time that he began to develop a passion for spiritualism, which he abandoned as soon as he came to recognize the truth of Christianity.

At the age of nineteen, he moved to Sergiev Posad (the religious center of Russia, forty-five miles northeast of Moscow), where he studied philosophy and theology at the Spiritual Academy for a year. It was there, surrounded by Greek Fathers and German philosophers, that his love for his cousin Katya Romanov, two years his junior, began to blossom. But this love match was doomed to fail: Vladimir saw marriage as self-denial and sacrifice, which Katya did not begin to accept.

Reading the letters he wrote to Katya, one realizes that Soloviev, who was only nineteen years old, already had an extremely precise vision of his vital mission: to create a philosophical system that would make it possible to understand the Christian faith in a modern context, to give theology a philosophical basis that could be understood by modern man.

Soloviev did not aspire to the monastic life. "Monastic life," he wrote, "once had a high significance, but the time has come not to flee the world but to go into it and transform it."[3]

At the age of twenty-one, in St. Petersburg, Soloviev defended his master's thesis on the crisis of Western philosophy. It was a complete success. He was made a lecturer at the University of Moscow.

He became friends with Professor Pamphil Yurkevich, who had a great influence on him. Like the biblical authors, Yurkevich saw the heart as the center of the personality. He protested against modern intellectualism, which considers "thought" the center of the soul. The essence of man, Yurkevich believed, is not thought, but the life of his heart, his immediate and deep feelings. Spiritual life is born in the darkness of the heart before taking shape in the light of reason. Intelligence is the summit, not the source, of spiritual life.

At the age of twenty-two, Soloviev was sent on a research mission abroad. He visited England, Egypt, Italy, and France. In England, he became familiar with mystical doctrines (the theology of Jacob Böhme and the Jewish Kabbalah, in particular).

First in The British Museum and then in the Egyptian desert, he had mystical experiences that were to serve as the starting point for his philosophy: "I saw it

---

3. Soloviev, С. Соловьёв, *Жизнь и творческая эволюция Владимира Соловьёва*, стр. 120 (*Vladimir Solovyov: His Life and Creative Evolution*) (1977), p. 120.

all, and all I saw was one."[4] Sophia (Wisdom), that mysterious being who embodies the unitotality of space and time—a concept closely associated with Soloviev—and who manifested herself to him, became the central theme of his thought.

Of this journey he will only remember The British Museum and the Egyptian desert. "I will never travel again,"[5] he wrote to his father from Paris. He did not leave Russia again until ten years later, in 1886.

Soloviev returned to Moscow a convinced Slavophile. In his short speech "Three Forces," delivered at a meeting of the Society of Lovers of Russian Literature, he set forth his credo: the East, which proclaims a divinity deprived of humanity, is the bearer of a first force; the West, which proclaims a humanity deprived of divinity, is the bearer of a second force; the Slavic world and Russia are the bearers of a third force, both human and divine.

> Our people's assumption of the appearances of a slave and the miserable state of the Russian economy not only do not contradict her vocation, but rather confirm it. For that higher power, which the Russian people are called to inject into humanity, is a power not of this world. Here material affluence counts for nothing.[6]

---

4. V. Soloviev, "Three Encounters," trans. Judith Deutsch Kornblatt, in *Divine Sophia: The Writings of Vladmir Solovyov*, ed. Judith Deutsch Kornblatt (Ithaca: Cornell University Press, 2009), p. 271.

5. Soloviev, С. Соловьёв, *Жизнь и творческая эволюция Владимира Соловьёва*, стр. 100 *(Vladimir Solovyov: His Life and Creative Evolution)* (1977), p. 100.n.

6. V. Soloviev, *Three Forces* (1877).

At the age of twenty-four, not wishing to take sides in a conflict between professors, Soloviev gave up his chair at Moscow University. He moved to St. Petersburg to become a member of the Scientific Committee of the Ministry of Education and taught at the city's main university. He met Dostoyevsky, thirty-two years his senior, and they became friends. Soon they made a pilgrimage together to the Optina Monastery, one of the most important spiritual centers of nineteenth-century Russia, located 155 miles southwest of Moscow.

In 1877, Soloviev met Sophie Khitrovo, who became his muse. In 1896, after the death of her husband, Soloviev proposed marriage. She refused.

In 1878, Soloviev gave his famous *Lectures on Godmanhood*.

The death of his father in 1879 affected him deeply. His piety became stronger.

In 1880, he defended his doctoral thesis, "Critique of Abstract Principles," at the University of St. Petersburg. "Abstract principles" are partial ideas separated from the whole and alienated from the "unitotality." Soloviev sought to reincorporate these principles, which in themselves carry a certain truth, into a unitary whole. He wanted to work for their return to living unity.

As a certain Professor Mikhail Vladislavtsev, who was very influential at the time, openly despised Soloviev, the latter did not obtain the title of professor; he remained a lecturer.

Dostoyevsky died on February 9, 1881, aged fifty-nine. A month later, Tsar Alexander II was assassinated by revolutionaries. On March 28, 1881, Soloviev called on his successor—Tsar Alexander III—to pardon the murderers in the name of Christian mercy. The government's response was immediate: Soloviev was banned from giving public lectures.

In 1882, Soloviev gave up even private teaching. He was twenty-nine years old. Thus ended the first period of the philosopher's life: speculative and experimental in his search for truth, combined with adherence to the Slavophile worldview and its struggle against rationalism, materialism, positivism, and atheism. A new, more practical, more journalistic, and, above all, more universal, period began: Soloviev attacked nationalism head-on, broke with the Slavophiles, drew closer to Catholicism, and actively worked for Christian unity.

Unity, love, communion . . . In everything he sought to achieve a synthesis: a synthesis of the human and the divine, the spiritual and the material; a synthesis of East and West, of Russia and Europe, of Orthodoxy and Catholicism. If Dostoyevsky was a primarily analytical mind, Soloviev was a fundamentally synthetic mind. According to the Catholic theologian Hans Urs von Balthasar, no one since Thomas Aquinas had possessed so brilliantly synthetic a mind.[7]

Beginning in 1886, Soloviev resumed his travels, visiting Zagreb, Paris, Scotland, and Egypt.

In 1891, his works were banned from publication in Russia. *Russia and the Universal Church* (an apologetic work

---

7. H. Urs von Balthasar, *Herrlichkeit: Eine Theologishe Ästhetik* (*The Glory of the Lord: A Theological Aesthetics*) (1962), vol. 2, part 2, p. 651, translation from German.

in defense of the primacy of the apostle Peter and his successor, the Bishop of Rome) was published in French in Paris.

In the 1890s, Soloviev returned to theoretical philosophy (*Beauty in Nature*; *The Meaning of Love*; *The Justification of the Good*).

In 1894, in Finland, where he lived, Soloviev had a premonition of a world cataclysm: "The insistent voice reverberates, without reproach, in the silence: / The end is near, the unexpected is about to happen."[8]

He was haunted by dark visions. He often saw the devil. In the summer of 1897, he wrote to his friend Velichko: "There is confusion, / My dreams are no longer the same, / Something is brewing, / Somebody is coming."[9]

The advent of the Antichrist had been on Soloviev's mind for a long time: as a child he mortified his body in order to strengthen his will in anticipation of the torments the Antichrist would inflict on Christians.

In the spring of 1899, Soloviev wrote his *Three Conversations on War, Progress, and the End of Human History*. The book ends with the famous "Short Tale of the Antichrist," in which the author declares that the twentieth century will be "the epoch of the last great wars and revolutions" and announces the arrival, in the twenty-first century in a "United States of Europe,"

---

8. V. Soloviev, "Сон наяву" ["The waking dream*], (January 1895), https://www.culture.ru/poems/21968/son-nayavu, translation from Russian.

9. L. V. Shaposhnikova, "Явление странствующего рыцаря" ["The appearance of the knight errant"*], Международный Центр Рерихов, https://icr.su/rus/about/direction/director/solovjev/04.php, translation from Russian.

of a "remarkable man" who will write a book that will advocate for deeply Christian values but will not mention the name of Christ anywhere.[10] The book will be a resounding success. The "remarkable man" who writes it is, of course, the Antichrist, with his plan to subsume Christianity into secular humanism. The "Short Tale of the Antichrist" would later become one of the favorite readings of Popes John Paul II and Benedict XVI.

In the summer of 1900, Soloviev traveled to Moscow to see to the publication of his translation of Plato's works. On July 15—the feast of St. Vladimir the Great, his name day—he fell ill. He was suffering from the effects of arterial sclerosis and cirrhosis of the liver, but the philosopher was stricken with an inexplicable new ailment that took him to his death bed. Soloviev was convinced that his illness was the devil's punishment for his Short Tale. He was only forty-seven years old.

He found refuge in the property occupied by his pupil and friend Sergei Trubetskoy, a professor at Moscow University. He confessed his sins and received Communion. Then he implored Trubetskoy's wife, "Keep me awake, force me to pray for the Jewish people, I must pray for them." He recited psalms in Hebrew aloud.

On August 13, 1900, he passed away after pronouncing his last words: "God's work is hard!"[11] He is buried in the cemetery of the Novodevichy monastery in Moscow, next to the grave of his father, Sergei.

---

10. V. Soloviev, "Short Tale of the Antichrist."

11. Soloviev, С. Соловьёв, *Жизнь и творческая эволюция Владимира Соловьёва*, стр. 210 (*Vladimir Solovyov: His Life and Creative Evolution*) (1977), p. 210.

Soloviev's Personality

Josip Strossmayer, the Croatian Catholic bishop and friend of Soloviev, in a letter of 1886 addressed to Serafino Vannutelli, apostolic nuncio in Vienna, declared: "Soloviev is a pure, pious and truly holy soul."[12]

Although he assimilated German philosophy, Christian theology, and Jewish Kabbalah by the age of twenty-three and brilliantly defended his master's thesis, Soloviev did not succumb to vanity:

> When in the dried mud
> I received the seed of truth,
> It sprouted and in haste,
> I gathered the first harvest.
> It was not I who made it grow and tended it,
> Who watered it with rain,
> Who made fresh air blow over it,
> Or warmed it with ardent rays.
> Not at all! In the thorns and brambles
> I was treading on the seedling of heaven,
> By the chaff of earthly ambitions,
> I was squeezing her and choking her.[13]

Soloviev was no armchair philosopher. He was a man of action fully aware of the sorrows and the needs

---

12. In Latin: "Solovief anima candida, pia ac vere santa est." Soloviev, С. Соловьёв, *Жизнь и творческая эволюция Владимира Соловьёва*, стр. 105 (*Vladimir Solovyov: His Life and Creative Evolution*) (1977), p. 105.

13. Soloviev, С. Соловьёв, *Жизнь и творческая эволюция Владимира Соловьёва*, стр. 150 (*Vladimir Solovyov: His Life and Creative Evolution*) (1977), p. 150.

of his time. A citizen in the broadest sense of the term, he was constantly concerned with questions of practical justice. He was interested in and wrote about everything. He was a universal man. If justice is the virtue of universality, as the ancient Greeks taught us, we can affirm, with the poet Vyacheslav Ivanov, that "justice was the specific virtue of Soloviev, the man of action and Soloviev, the philosopher. The justice that Soloviev practiced was marked by a pious attention to everything, a joyful embrace of all reality."[14]

One could write a treatise on Soloviev's fortitude. No one doubted his courage when, in his master's thesis, he attacked positivism, the religion of the intellectuals of the time. The Slavophiles supported him at first, but soon abandoned him: they could not forgive his sharp criticism of nationalism, his aspirations for a universal Christianity, or his attempts to explain Christian doctrine by means of new philosophical concepts adapted to the needs of the modern world. "Soloviev," wrote the philosopher and theologian Sergei Bulgakov, "raised his flag high and boldly when it required true heroism to do so. The valiant crusader found no compassion or understanding in either of the two camps that divided the society of the time."[15]

---

14. V. Ivanov, В. Иванов. О значении Вл. Соловьева в судьбах нашего религиозного сознания [On the importance of V. Soloviev in the destiny of our religious consciousness*] (1911), p. 130, translation form Russian.

15. S. Bulgakov. С. Булгаков, С. Что дает современному сознанию философия Вл. Соловьева [The contribution of the philosophy of V. Soloviev to modern consciousness*] (1903), p. 150, translation from Russian.

In the 1880s Soloviev was alone, abandoned by all. In one of his poems of 1882 on the theme of Christmas, we find this verse: "Poor child, between two enemy camps, for You there is no shelter."[16]

The blows dealt by the Russian state did not make him bitter but enkindled in him a combative zeal. In 1886, he wrote to his sister Nadia: "I must walk before the Lord, and not strut before the crowd on my hind legs."[17]

For Soloviev, Christ is the heart of his doctrine and his life. In his *Lectures on Godmanhood* (1877–1881), he wrote: "The originality of Christianity is not in its speculative content but in its personal incarnation. . . . The content of Christianity is Christ, only and exclusively Christ. In Christianity as such we find Christ and only Christ."[18]

In 1884, Soloviev published his *Spiritual Foundations of Life*. This book, which deals with important Christian topics such as prayer, sacrifice, charity, the sacraments, the Church, the state, and society, ends with a brief essay entitled "The Figure of Christ as an Examination of Conscience." Here, Soloviev gives the reader some advice: Before any important action, remember Christ, contemplate him, and ask yourself—would he have acted in this way? Everyone should make this

---

16. V. Soloviev, "Собрание стихотворений" ["Collection of poems*], Lib.ru Classic, July 2007, http://az.lib.ru/s/solowxew_wladimir_sergeewich/text_0060.shtml#030, translation from Russian.

17. Soloviev, С. Соловьёв, *Жизнь и творческая эволюция Владимира Соловьёва*, стр. 128 (*Vladimir Solovyov: His Life and Creative Evolution*) (1977), p. 128.

18. V. Soloviev, *Lectures on Godmanhood* (1877–1881), lecture 5.

examination of conscience; no one will be disappointed. In case of doubt, remember Christ, imagine him alive, as he is, and place on him the burden of your doubts.

Under the influence of Soloviev, a very important part of the Russian intelligentsia abandoned Marxism for Christianity, which served as the starting point for the philosophical and religious renaissance of the early twentieth century.[19] Vyacheslav Ivanov, who a few years later, during his emigration, would coin the beautiful phrase "the two lungs of Christianity" (referring to the East and the West), would never forget his last meeting with Soloviev. It was a decisive turning point for him: it marked his return to the Church of Christ. "Only God knows," writes the theologian Mikhail Aksionov-Meerson, "how many people owe Soloviev their conversion. Only God knows how many he has brought to Christ by his pen and the testimony of his life, and how many more he will bring."[20]

Soloviev's Mystical Experience

Soloviev's mystical experiences led him to conceive of the universe as a living organism whose unity is ensured by an invisible creature he called Sophia—Wisdom.

In the Greek patristic tradition, Sophia is the Word of God, the Second Person of the Holy Trinity,

---

19. The Russian Religious Renaissance was a period from roughly 1880 to 1950, which witnessed a great creative outpouring of Russian philosophy, theology, and spirituality. The term is derived from the title of a 1963 book by Nicholas Zernov, *The Russian Religious Renaissance of the Twentieth Century*.

20. M. Meerson-Aksenov, Михаил Аксенов-Меерсон, Соловьев в наши дни [Soloviev today*], p. 140, translation from Russian.

the uncreated Wisdom. The Book of Proverbs, however, speaks to us of a Uncreated wisdom, a mediator of Creation:

> The LORD brought me forth as the first of his works,
>   before his deeds of old;
> I was formed long ages ago,
>   at the very beginning, when the world came to be. . . .
> I was there when he set the heavens in place. . . .
> Then I was constantly at his side.
> I was filled with delight day after day,
>   rejoicing always in his presence.[21]

This mediatrix of Creation is traditionally perceived as a feminine principle. This "eternal feminine" (to use Goethe's expression) is embodied in a particular way in the Mother of God. Sophiology is intimately linked to Mariology. If, in Constantinople, the Church of Hagia Sophia is dedicated to Christ, in Russia, the feast of the churches dedicated to Sophia is celebrated on the liturgical feasts of the Mother of God (in Kiev on the feast of the Nativity of Mary, in Novgorod and elsewhere on the feast of the Dormition).

"The figure of wisdom (Sophia) was probably derived from Egyptian prototypes and then adapted to Israel's beliefs," writes Joseph Ratzinger (the future Pope Benedict XVI).

> Wisdom appears as the mediatrix of creation and salvation history, as God's first creature, in whom both the pure, primordial form of his creative will and the pure *answer*, which he discovers, find their

---

21. Prv 8:22–23, 27, 30 (NIV).

expression. . . . Creation answers, and the answer is as close to God as a playmate, as a lover. . . . [The relation between the Wisdom books and Mary] has been sharply criticized by this century's liturgical movement . . . It has been argued that these texts can and should allow only a christological interpretation. After years of wholehearted agreement with this latter view, it is ever clear to me that it actually misjudges what is most characteristic in those Wisdom texts. . . . In both Hebrew and Greek, "wisdom" is a feminine noun. . . . a feminine noun, stands on that side of reality which is represented by the woman, by what is purely and simply feminine. It signifies the answer which emerges from the divine call of creation and election. It expresses precisely this: that there is a pure answer and that God's love finds its irrevocable dwelling place within it. . . . Sophia refers to the Logos, the Word who establishes wisdom, and also to the womanly answer which receives wisdom and brings it to fruition. The eradication of the Marian interpretation of sophiology ultimately leaves out an entire dimension of the biblical and Christian mystery. . . . The figure of the woman . . . expresses the reality of creation, as well as the fruitfulness of grace. . . . Mary emerges as the personal epitome of the feminine principle. . . . To deny or reject the feminine aspect in belief, or, more concretely, the Marian aspect, leads finally to the negation of creation and the invalidation of grace.[22]

---

22. J. Ratzinger, *Daughter Zion: Meditations on the Church's Marian Belief* (San Francisco: Ignatius, 1983), pp. 25–28

Sophia, as a feminine principle mysteriously linked to the Creation of the world and the Redemption of humanity, is not an esoteric concept but a Christian reality confirmed by Holy Scripture and the most solid theology.

In his autobiographical poem "Three Encounters" of 1898, written two years before his death, Soloviev recounts what he calls his "appointments" with Sophia. These are mystical experiences that are, in his own words, "the most significant moments of my life."[23]

Let us analyze this poem.

At the age of nine, young Vladimir fell in love with a girl who, unfortunately for him, preferred another boy. This led to an infantile drama replete with all the twists and turns of grand passion (he even "challenged" his rival to a duel), but it also led to Soloviev's "first encounter" with the heavenly Friend, Sophia. On Ascension Day 1862, in church, when the choir intoned the Hymn of the Cherubim, she made her appearance. The flow of passions instantly faded in the soul of the young boy:

> . . . the azure round about, the azure in my soul
> Suffused with golden azure,
> Holding in your hand a flower from another world,
> You stood there with a radiant smile,
> You nodded and disappeared in the cloud.

The "second encounter" occurred thirteen years later—Soloviev was twenty-two years old—in the reading room of the British Museum:

---

23. Soloviev, "Author's note" concluding "Three Encounters," trans. Judith Deutsch Kornblatt, in *Divine Sophia*, p. 272.

> Suddenly everything is filled with a golden azure,
> And before me she shone once more—
> But only her face—it alone.
>
> I said to her: your face appears before me,
> But I now wish to behold all of you. . . .
>
> "Then be in Egypt!" cried a voice within me.

The "third encounter" occurred shortly afterward, in the Egyptian desert:

> And in the purple of heaven's splendor,
> With eyes filled with an azure fire,
> You looked about like the first radiance
> Of creation's universal day of days.
>
> What is, what was, whatever will be—
> Was there embraced in one motionless gaze. . . .
>
> I saw it all, and all I saw was one.
> A single image of all female beauty.
> The immeasurable encompassing its sum.
> Before me, in me—were you alone.
>
> O, radiant woman! In you I am not deceived:
> In the desert I saw all of you . . .
> Those roses will not wither in my soul
> Wherever life's torrent may lead me.[24]

---

24. Soloviev, "Three Encounters," trans. Judith Deutsch Kornblatt, in *Divine Sophia*, pp. 270–271, with some translation changes made by the author.

Three times in his life the young Soloviev felt the proximity of Sophia, who embodied for him the unitotality: "I saw it all, and all I saw was one. A single image of all female beauty."

Soloviev's Sophia, according to one scholar of his thought,

> is an individual being, concrete, alive, almost tangible and in any case accessible to the sight, a divine-human being, human in feminine form, a close and condescending being accessible in intellectual, personal and direct communion, understanding and addressing the word, a being that helps and guides in life, a being finally, that is loved with a lively and ardent love, sublimated, certainly, and purified of all sensuality, but nevertheless conscious of being addressed to a feminine being that accepts it, perhaps answers it and rewards it in any case by revealing her beauty, which is never an abstract beauty.[25]

Soloviev's philosophical thought is based on a personal mystical experience. Unitotality is not an abstract idea for him, but an experienced reality.

Soloviev was gifted with an exceptional sensitivity that he inherited from his mother. He deeply felt the unity of the created world. Through his heart he perceived "the first radiance of creation's universal day of days," the created wisdom unifying in it all the parts of the cosmos.

---

25. A. Kojevnikoff, "La métaphysique religieuse de Vladimir Soloviev" ["Vladmir Soloviev's religious metaphysics"*], *Revue d'histoire et de philosophie religieuses* 15, nos. 1–2 (January–April 1935), pp. 110–152, translation from French.

"The branches of the tree," he writes, "cross, mingle and touch each other. . . . Such is external knowledge; but these same branches also communicate with each other through their common trunk and their roots from which they receive life. Such is mystical knowledge."[26]

Soloviev is a religious philosopher in the sense that mystical experience is the basis of his philosophical system. The mystical intuition of unitotality that his poetry transmits to us produces the rational ideas of his philosophy. For Soloviev, the mysticism of the heart, unable to translate its intimate movements into abstract, solid, scientific concepts—into food for the intelligence—contradicts the very nature of the human mind.[27]

In Soloviev, the deepest mysticism coexists with the highest rationality. His Sophiology, as he expounds it, is, however, extremely complicated and confusing. Some experts claim to find contradictions in it. It should be kept in mind, however, that these are not flaws in Soloviev's exposition of his idea so much as difficulties inherent in the idea itself. In any case, a deep exposition of his Sophiology is beyond the scope of this book.

The Philosophy of Unitotality

For Soloviev, the unitotality of the universe is compromised by original sin. The universe is no longer cosmos

---

26. V. Soloviev, В. Соловьёв, Собр. соч. СПб., 1911–1914. Т.1. С.186 [Collected works*] (St. Petersburg, 1901–1903), vol. 2, p. 314, translation from Russian.

27. Soloviev, В. Соловьёв [Collected works*], vol. 1, p. 186.

(order), but chaos, whose separate and isolated elements nevertheless continue to aspire to unity. Unitotality (unity in multiplicity) is a long process of recapitulation and reunification. It is also the goal of universal history.

"For Soloviev," writes Nicolas Berdyaev,

> by moving away from God, the world disintegrates, divides into enemy parts. Egotistical self-affirmation and the resulting alienation are the clearest signs of the fall of man and the world. But each part separated from the center contains within it a part of the truth, a partial truth. To reunite these parts by submitting them to God is to achieve unitotality.[28]

Soloviev calls abstract principles the particular ideas that selfishly assert themselves in their particularity. These ideas are false, but they contain important truths that should not be denied but rather be supplemented by other truths no less important.

Soloviev, for example, recognizes in each philosophical system a partial truth, which must be completed by other truths that the partial truth does not know.

Thus, atheistic humanism is an error (the denial of God) which contains a partial truth (faith in humanity). To overcome atheistic humanism, it is necessary to elaborate a doctrine in which faith in humanity is rooted in faith in God.

---

28. N. Berdiaev, Н. Бердяев, Русская идея [The Russian idea] (Paris, 1946), translation from Russian, https://nnov.hse.ru/data/2018/02/20/1165426589/Бердяев%20Николай.%20Русская%20идея%20-%20royallib.ru.pdf.

Soloviev asserts that the truth of naturalism is its admiration for human nature and its high capacities; its error is to deny the existence of original sin, our tendency toward evil, and the necessity of grace in salvation. To overcome naturalism is to affirm with "realistic optimism" the incredible potential of human nature without, however, closing our eyes to the limitations caused by the original wound.

The truth of liberalism, comparatively, is to exalt freedom; its error is its indifference to truth. To overcome liberalism is to proclaim freedom in a constant search for truth.

The truth of socialism is to emphasize the social nature of man; its error is to deny his individuality. To overcome socialism is to realize a social policy that respects the individuality of people.

The truth of nationalism he continues, is to affirm the particularity and proper mission of each nation; its error is to deny the solidarity of the human race. To overcome nationalism is to choose the path of a patriotism that contributes to the good of the whole human family.

To *overcome*, according to the principles of the Hegelian dialectic, is to arrive at a synthesis of the positive aspects of both the thesis and the antithesis.

Soloviev applies the principle of unitotality to religion. In his Third Speech in "Three Speeches on Dostoevsky" delivered on February 19, 1883, he asserts that Russia's centuries of struggle with the non-Christian East and the Christian West have served to build up a powerful Russian state apparatus. Now that the state's physical strength is an undeniable reality, Russia must show its spiritual strength by working for the unity of Christianity. Russia's mission is to achieve a synthesis of the thesis of national chauvinism and its antithesis—cosmopolitanism, the globalism of Soloviev's day. It is the affirmation of religious unity in cultural multiplicity.

For Soloviev, Divine Providence allowed the separation between the Orthodox Church and the Catholic Church in order to achieve a greater good: to allow the Church of Christ to discover in herself all the human and divine richness of the Incarnation and Redemption. "For human knowledge and human action," writes Pope John Paul II,

> a certain dialectic is present. Didn't the Holy Spirit, in his divine "condescendence," take this into consideration? It is necessary for humanity to achieve unity through plurality, to learn to come together in the one Church, even while presenting a plurality of ways of thinking and acting, of cultures and civilizations. Wouldn't such a way of looking at things be, in a certain sense, more consonant with the wisdom of God, with His goodness and providence? Nevertheless, this cannot be a justification for the divisions that continue to deepen! The time must come for the love that unites us to be manifested![29]

Vladimir Soloviev was the first—a century before John Paul II—to pose the question of Christian unity in dialectical terms; that is, in terms of unitotality.

---

29. John Paul II, *Crossing the Threshold of Hope* (New York: Alfred A. Knopf, 1994), chap. 23, p. 153

The Theology of Godmanhood

Soloviev's doctrine of Godmanhood refers to the union without confusion and without separation of the human and divine natures of Jesus Christ. This faithfully echoes the Council of Chalcedon of 451.

In Soloviev's opinion, without the Incarnation of the Divinity in matter, the world, like mankind, would be devoid of meaning. Soloviev is convinced that God would have become man, even if man had not sinned. God became flesh for us men, as we affirm in the Creed, and not only for our salvation.

> The incarnation of the Divine is not a miracle in the proper sense of the word, i.e., it is not something foreign to the general order of things. On the contrary, it is something essentially related to the whole history of humanity, something prepared by this history, and which proceeds logically from it. . . . The personal incarnation of the Word in an individual man is the last link in a long series of other incarnations, physical and historical. This manifestation of God in human flesh is the most perfect and complete theophany in the line of other theophanies—incomplete, preparative, and transformative. From this point of view, the apparition of the spiritual man, the birth of the second Adam, is not less understandable than the apparition of the natural man on earth, the birth of the first Adam. Both are, in a sense, the fruit of a miracle. But this new event without precedent was prepared by everything that preceded it—all of nature anticipated and aspired

to the coming of man, all the history of humanity was directed towards the God-Man. . . . The incarnation of the Divinity is not only possible—it participates essentially in the general plan of creation.[30]

To assert that the Incarnation proceeds logically from human history is not to deny that it was a completely gratuitous act of God.

The Incarnation is the central event of the cosmic and historical process. Theandry—that is, the union of the divine and the human (and through it, of the whole of creation)—must be realized in the fullness of space and time. The Church, which is "humanity reunited with its divine principle through Jesus Christ,"[31] is the privileged instrument of the theandric process. All that is earthly must be divinized. The kingdom of God toward which humanity is striving is the result of this divinization.

If, according to Soloviev, medieval Christianity insufficiently respected the human principle, contemporary civilization insufficiently respects the divine principle. Nevertheless, by forcefully affirming the human principle and all that proceeds from it (notably human rights), atheistic humanism participates actively, albeit unconsciously, in the theandric process and in the promotion of Christianity. The Church is the center of this process, but this process encompasses the whole

---

30. Soloviev, *Lectures on Godmanhood* (1877–1881), lectures 11 and 12.

31. Soloviev, *Lectures on Godmanhood* (1877–1881), lecture 10.

history of humanity, including that of non-Christian or anti-Christian civilizations.

The essence of Christianity, Soloviev asserts, is the transformation of the world and of humanity in the spirit of Christ. This transformation is a slow and complex process. The kingdom of God is a tree that grows, fruit that ripens, dough that rises.

The majority of the early Christians believed that the kingdom of God was a material and imminent reality, the result of a physical miracle (the return of Christ) that was to happen in their "today." Despite the heroism of their lives, their vision of the kingdom of God was fundamentally one of "consolation."

When pagans converted to Christianity in the fourth century, it was the idea of "individual salvation" that attracted them above all. The important thing for them was to save their souls and those of others, not to save society and the world by Christianizing them. On the contrary, they fled from the world and society. The preaching of the great saints of the Middle Ages, especially in the East (with the exception of St. John Chrysostom and a few others), hardly ever touched on the reform of social structures.

According to Soloviev, it even seems that, by renouncing the world narrowly conceived as society, the Christians of the Middle Ages also renounced the world understood as the realm of matter in the broad sense. Eastern dualism (spiritualism) came back in force, incompatible with the very foundations of Christianity, which is the religion of the Incarnation and of the resurrection of the flesh.

Where, then, did all the social progress of the preceding centuries down to the present day come from? Relatively few of those who fought for progress considered themselves Christians. If "nominal" Christians can be said to have betrayed the work of Christ, why can't "nominal" non-Christians (the French Jacobins, for example) be said to have served it? The abolition of torture, serfdom, persecution of heretics—all these seem to have been the work of non-believers. It could well be that our godless social engineers—some of them, at any rate—have unwittingly contributed to the building of a Christian society.[32]

The world has been in the hands of non-Christians for several centuries. They are the ones who are advancing civilization. But how far can they go in their project without God? Can a godless civilization even survive?

> Though the revolutionary movement destroyed many things that needed to be destroyed, though it swept away many an injustice and swept it away forever, it nevertheless failed lamentably in the attempt to create a social order founded upon justice. Justice is simply the practical expression and application of truth; and the revolutionary movement's point of departure was falsehood. The declaration of the Rights of Man could only provide a positive principle for social reconstruction if it were based upon a true conception of Man himself. That of the revolutionaries is

---

32. V. Soloviev, В. Соловьёв, "Об упадке средневекового миросозерцания" [On the decline of the medieval worldview] (1891), translation from Russian, https://www.vehi.net/soloviev/upadok.html.

well-known: they perceived in Man nothing but abstract individuality, a rational being devoid of all positive content. I do not propose . . . to show how this abstract "Man" was suddenly transformed into the no less abstract "Citizen," how the free, sovereign individual found himself doomed to be the defenseless slave and victim of the absolute State or "Nation," that is to say, of a group of obscure persons borne to the surface of public life by the eddies of revolution and rendered the more ferocious by the consciousness of their own intrinsic inanity.[33]

If atheistic humanism has served the interests of Christianity by proclaiming certain Christian truths that Christians have forgotten, it is in its essence a lie that renders its own future null and void.

LIVING ACCORDING TO SOLOVIEV

To live according to Soloviev is to pay pious attention to everything: to all creatures and to all events; it is to give each person and every idea its due. It is to practice justice, which is the virtue of universality.

To live according to Soloviev is to seek unity in diversity. It is to reject sterile uniformity, while actively working for the unity and solidarity of the human family.

continued

---

33. V. Soloviev, *La Russie et l'Eglise Universelle* [Russia and the Universal Church] (Paris: F. X. de Guilbert, 2008), p. vii, translation from French.

> LIVING ACCORDING TO SOLOVIEV *continued*
>
> To live according to Soloviev is to overcome the barriers (physical, intellectual, cultural, and religious) that separate people, and to actively love (in the broadest sense of the term), which is the virtue of communion and interdependence.
>
> To live according to Soloviev is to practice unity of life, to divinize all aspects of human existence, to sanctify the world by filling it with the Christian spirit, to build the kingdom of God at the very heart of society.

CONCLUSION

REASON, THE WILL, AND THE HEART are faculties intimately linked to each other. If one of them is isolated from the others, it becomes perverted and thus perverts the totality of the human organism: it produces deformed beings with deformed thoughts. In the context of a civilization obsessed by the idea of "Progress," deformity, and even monstrosity has a leg up and is bound to succeed. The rationalist Descartes is the father of the subjectivism and moral relativism that have invaded all spheres of contemporary culture. The sentimentalist Rousseau is the founder of a new religion of a sociopolitical nature that has conquered the hearts of millions of our contemporaries. The voluntarist Nietzsche is the spiritual guide of an ever-increasing army of power-hungry psychopaths and maniacs.

Subjectivism and relativism in the realm of reason; sentimentality, Hollywood values, and woke ideology in the realm of the heart; totalitarianism and terrorism in the realm of the will—that is the world we are living in.

Unlike these *partial* personalities with partial philosophies, Pascal, Kierkegaard, Dostoyevsky, and Soloviev are *integral* personalities, each developing in his own way an integral philosophy. Their hearts, their minds, and their wills work in unison.

Beyond their shared anthropology, what unites Pascal, Kierkegaard, Dostoyevsky, and Soloviev is the light of the Christian faith. This light allows them to accurately identify the vices of our civilization and to offer the world pathways to salvation. Pascal, Kierkegaard, Dostoyevsky, and Soloviev understood an obvious fact, which the world has been trying to ignore for centuries: if we want to save humanity, we must "save" God, because man without God is nothing.

In the Russians—Dostoyevsky and Soloviev—what is most striking is the insight and precision with which they foresaw the upheavals we are experiencing today. "The Legend of the Grand Inquisitor" (1879) and the "Short Tale of the Antichrist" (1899) are works of surprising timeliness.

The Grand Inquisitor and the Antichrist present themselves as "humanists," but deep down they have nothing but contempt for humanity. This is the great lie of the modern age. Modern evil is more subtle than the old evil. Previously, evil was clearer and simpler. The "bad guys" in Hollywood movies looked like bad guys. Now, they look like good guys and talk about Progress, Liberation, Tolerance, and Love!

In the name of love—love of neighbor!—the new inquisitors, including no shortage of "church people," are today embarked on a frantic race to "lighten" Christian morality, and even to undermine the basic principles of natural morality. Having lost their faith, they reject the love of God and have become fanatics of the love of neighbor (they want to "free" people from the "burden" of conscience). Everything happens here just as in Dostoyevsky's work: *in the name of the love of man, men are turned into trained poodles.*

Christianity, moreover, tends to be reduced more and more to a vague, humanistic, and philanthropic feeling, whose highest objective is to be "nice to everyone." We are abandoning Christ and his sacraments. Everything is taking place as in Soloviev's writings: *secular humanism absorbs Christianity and replaces it without anyone realizing what's happening.*

Man is only a poodle, but he is nice to everyone—to all the other poodles! Transcendence is repealed, socialization is the name of the game. Impiety toward God and humanistic fanaticism toward men—all in a context of excessive sensitivity and pseudo-religiosity. Horizontal man, man flat on his back—such are the times we live in. It is the biggest lie humanity has ever known. Perhaps the last one.

Dostoyevsky and Soloviev open our eyes to the times we are living in. They encourage us to make radical choices, to live this "apocalypse" with wisdom, audacity, and magnanimity. Soloviev shows us the way: the Woman clothed with the sun, with the moon under her feet and a crown of twelve stars on her head. The Sophia who lovingly gathers her scattered children and reunites the dislocated parts of the universe. The Mediatrix of Creation and Redemption, the Ark of Salvation.